"These narratives spea[k] queer folks and their f[amilies] through disclosures an[d] invite others to get to know them anew. These relationships are ever-changing and significant as families of origin and choice recognize their beloveds, wrestle with the meaning of their lives together, and become open to transformation. The writers beautifully speak to the pains and the celebrations of queer people whose resilient spirits have much to offer to communities and the world."

— JORETTA L. MARSHALL

professor of pastoral theology and care at Brite Divinity School

"Hays and Chiasson have assembled a fascinating and forceful collection of stories from LGBTQ+ Christians about their experiences with kinship and condemnation, love and loss, reconciliation and resilience, and coming out—and coming to terms with one's queer self. An engaging, well-theorized, and well-researched text that calls cis-het Christians to lean in, listen, and believe; a text that will make a marked contribution toward repairing the harms that Christian families, faiths, and fellowships have inflicted (and still inflict) on LGBTQ+ persons."

— TONY E. ADAMS

chair and professor of communication at Bradley University
and author of *Narrating the Closet*

FAMILY OF ORIGIN, FAMILY OF CHOICE

Stories of Queer Christians

KATIE HAYS
AND **SUSAN A. CHIASSON**

WILLIAM B. EERDMANS PUBLISHING COMPANY

GRAND RAPIDS, MICHIGAN

Wm. B. Eerdmans Publishing Co.
4035 Park East Court SE, Grand Rapids, Michigan 49546
www.eerdmans.com

27 26 25 24 23 22 21   1 2 3 4 5 6 7

ISBN 978-0-8028-7857-1

Library of Congress Cataloging-in-Publication Data

Names: Hays, Katie, 1969– author. | Chiasson, Susan A.,
    1954– author.
Title: Family of origin, family of choice : stories of queer Christians /
    Katie Hays and Susan A. Chiasson.
Description: Grand Rapids, Michigan : William B. Eerdmans Pub-
    lishing Company, 2021. | Summary: "A collection of first-person
    narratives from LGBTQ+ Christians about navigating their
    family relationships after coming out"—Provided by publisher.
Identifiers: LCCN 2020049006 | ISBN 9780802878571
Subjects: LCSH: Sexual minorities—Religious life. | Sexual minori-
    ties—Biography. | Sexual minorities—Family relationships.
Classification: LCC BV4596.G38 H39 2021 | DDC 248.8086/6—dc23
LC record available at https://lccn.loc.gov/2020049006

Unless otherwise noted, Scripture quotations are from the New
Revised Standard Version of the Bible.

CONTENTS

CONTENTS

REFLECTIONS AND CONCLUSIONS

FOREWORD

Once, I directed a national church-planting ministry and also preached in several of America's largest churches. But when I came out as transgender, I lost every single one of my jobs and most of my friends. Overnight I had become a pariah, a supposed danger to the church and her purposes. I was devastated. I had been with the ministry for thirty-five years. I never had a bad job review, and the growth we experienced was steady and strong. Yet I was gone within seven short days after coming out, ostracized from the denomination my family has been a part of for generations, stripped of my pension, and left without a church home, the place I served as a teaching pastor. It was the darkest chapter of my own complicated narrative.

In the evolution of our species, what brought humans together beyond the level of blood kin was not the need for safety but the need for meaning. Why are we on this earth and for what purpose? That is why we told stories around the campfire. We were driven by our collective desire to craft a compelling story. Our need for story is biological. We do not sleep without dreaming, and most people do not dream in mathematical equations; we dream in stories. In my work as a pastoral counselor, I often see a breakthrough arrive hidden within the narrative of a client's dream. A good story invites us to do the work of showing up. It bids us to create our own narrative instead of numbingly accepting the stories our culture prepackages for us.

All three Abrahamic religions—Judaism, Islam, and Christianity—are desert religions and as such were initially religions of scarcity. There was not an abundance of resources in the desert, so every community had to take care of its own. In their fundamentalist forms, all three religions remain religions of scarcity, believing a common enemy is necessary for the community to survive. Where no enemy exists, they create one. One of the enemies created by fundamentalist Christianity is the LGBTQ population. Though 48 percent of us identify as Christian, two-thirds of us are no longer welcome in our communities of faith.

Fortunately, I found a church in Denver that nurtured me back to health, and I now serve as one of the co-pastors at a sister church they helped start, Left Hand Church in Boulder County, Colorado. Thanks to a few well-received TED talks, I am also a frequent speaker on gender equity. Whether I am speaking in London or Louisville, I end all of my talks by saying, "The call toward authenticity is sacred, and holy, and for the greater good." Living authentically is not easy. Families are thrown into turmoil. Friendships are ripped apart. It takes courage to journey authentically. But it is worth it, because the authentic journey *is* sacred, and holy, and for the greater good.

Toward the end of my first TED talk, I told the story of my ninety-three-year-old father, an evangelical minister who struggled with my transition before graciously choosing to honor the journey of his child. Dad passed away recently, but our last few years together brought healing and reconciliation. What I did not mention in that first talk was that my mother never did accept me as Paula. She saw me twice after my transition but withheld any affirmation of my identity. As is so often the case when an LGBTQ person comes out in a nonaffirming family, there was no unqualified happy ending. My father accepted me; my mother did not. How does a family recover from that kind of trauma?

In *Family of Origin, Family of Choice: Stories of Queer Christians*, Katie Hays and Susan Chiasson have brought fifteen touching narratives to the pages of a vibrant and hopeful book. Fifteen generous souls from Galileo Church were interviewed by Susan and Katie and graciously allowed their stories to be told. These are stories of struggle and reconciliation, despair and hope, sorrow and joy. They are complex stories that emphasize the dignity of each person involved. There are no bad guys on these pages, only humans trying to make their way through difficult circumstances. When a family member comes out as LGBTQ, superficial family relationships rarely survive. Only those families willing to go through the chaos and emptiness of the dark night find their way to the new dawn. Some of the stories do not end as you might hope, but all of them are redemptive. Katie's and Susan's comments provide a clear path for families to embrace their loved ones who have risked everything to live authentically.

In the epic Greek poem *The Odyssey*, the journey of Odysseus was not finished when he returned to Ithaca. He accepted another journey, this time inland. He traveled until he came to a place in which people did not know an oar when they saw one. There he planted the oar he carried with him, an offering to the god Poseidon. Only then did Odysseus get to return home and live into sleek old age. Like Odysseus, we are all on a journey, maybe our first, maybe our last, but all into the unknown, undertaken when it would have been easier to sit on the couch binge-watching someone else's journey. But this living is serious business, and we are all pilgrims, called onto the road less traveled. And for all the uncertainty, we can know two things: The world can change for the better, but someone has to pay the price.

These stories are of people who paid the price. They sought reconciliation when it would have been easier to walk away. They did the hard work of showing up to love each other well. And they found a church willing to do the hard work with them. If you are moved by a good, redemptive story, you are going to like this book.

Paula Stone Williams (she/her)
Lyons, Colorado

PROLOGUE

Galileo Church, Our Family of Choice

The other day a cis-het, Gen X, formerly fundagelical, dear friend of ours sent a text that began, "Some of my gender-diverse friends and I were talking, and . . ." He wanted to tell us some new language those friends were using to refer to each other, as we are always learning how to honor our beloveds' identities in our hearts and in our conversations.

We paused for a moment in the text exchange to give thanks that we each know *lots* of LGBTQ+ humans who honor us with their friendship. We remember when we didn't know even one, and how much poorer our lives were for it. But God does not leave us where we were. "Thanks be to God," I (Katie) thumbed. "Indeed, thanks be to God," he texted back.

One of the ways God has moved the coauthors of this book along is by plopping us down on the path of faith alongside the gorgeous rainbow of Jesus-people known as Galileo Church. Galileo is a 2013 church plant on the southeast outskirts of Fort Worth, Texas. Our appreciation for the diversity of human identities runs deep, now. Our admiration for the gumption it takes to hang on to both queer identity *and* Christian faith is massive.

All the people whose stories we tell and reflect on in this book are Galileo co-conspirators, or Galileo friends, or Galileo-adjacent. They all trusted us enough to believe that we would do our best to do some good with their hearts' disclosures. We dedicate this book to them, their partners, their kids, and their families of origin (the good, the bad, and the ugly). It has been love's labor to listen and learn.

We are also deeply grateful to an anonymous donor whose enthusiasm for this project made it seem possible, and whose generosity made it actual.

This is Galileo Church's book, now. All the proceeds from its sale are for Galileo's life together. If there are flaws in the work, those are ours alone, and we'll hope for forgiveness from those who have given us so much already. If it generates any goodness in the world God still loves, you can safely give all the credit to Galileo Church, which will in turn give all the glory to God.

· INTRODUCTIONS ·

TELL US THE SHAPE OF YOUR SHALOM

The Pastor's Introduction

Katie Hays (she/her)

She covered her face with her hands as she wept. "I thought they would love me anyway," she said. "They always said blood was thicker than water, and family means sticking together, and all that crap. That's what it was—just crap." My young friend had screwed up her courage to bring her girlfriend home to her parents the year before, coming out with that introduction, and it had not gone well.

Over time things settled; her sister relayed the message that her parents were mellowing and she should try again to come home. "But don't bring anyone with you this time," her sister said. "We're okay with what you do in your home, but we can't have it here."

"Is this how it's gonna be for the rest of my life?" she asked me through her hands. "I have to hide my real life from my family so they can love the small part of me they can accept? Is it even worth it?"

Another day: he is visibly upset, knee bouncing manically from the ball of his foot, the furrow between his eyebrows seriously deep. "Look, this can't be on me," he said. "That sermon last Sunday, the one about forgiveness, and that thing where we write down who we need to forgive and dissolve it in the baptistery—*fuck* that. If that's what it takes to be a good Christian, I'm done."

A couple of years earlier his parents had forced him to unlock his phone, reading through his text messages to find evidence of the truth they didn't want to know. Their son was gay, so he couldn't be their son anymore, they said. He sofa-surfed among friends for a year or so and was finally in an apartment of his own, enough out of crisis mode to grieve the loss of relationship. This was the anger stage, for sure.

One more: they have big plans, these gender-diverse lovelies who are giddy with romance and ready to marry. But a conflict they can't resolve surfaces again and again. One of them has reached a tenuous truce with their extended family, allowing grandparents and assorted cousins to misgender and misname them for the sake of family calm. The other, for the sake of their hard-won emotional health, has cut ties with any person, relatives included, who won't get on board with their emerging identity.

So who will be on the guest list for the wedding? And for the long term, what will be the parameters for interaction with extended family on either side of the new family they are forming together? They're hopeful that I can adjudicate, and they've agreed to abide by whatever wisdom I offer.

Family of Origin, Family of Choice

Among the groan-worthy jokes that pastors and priests tell repeatedly is that old chestnut, "Seminary didn't prepare me for this." We say it while we're setting up tables and chairs for a potluck dinner, reading mechanical blueprints for the HVAC overhaul in an old sanctuary, or teaching another bookkeeping assistant the finer points of payroll administration.

Of course, the *actual* deficit in seminary training (by definition, because there is no adequate training for this) has to do with the infinite variety of human suffering that makes its way into our churches, our offices, and our lives. And so much of that suffering happens in the context of relationships between people who are meant to love each other the most. Loving someone means being vulnerable to that person, and vulnerable people are easily hurt. Even the most thorough theological education can't possibly prepare our hearts for all the ways that people can be hurt and all the ways people find to hurt each other, even when (or because) they love each other.

The subset of suffering-in-relationship that the LGBTQ+ community brings to the pastor's office (or back porch, or dinner table, or FaceTime screen) has called forth new understandings from me. When parents reject their gay child, or an extended family pressures their queer relative to conform or keep quiet, or a gender-diverse young adult keeps their identity secret to avoid loss of material support (college tuition, a place to live, health insurance—not small benefits, but how high the price?)—how am I meant to comfort, fortify, challenge, and bless in concert with the teachings of Jesus? What is the Christian community's most Christian response to the fracturing of families of origin around queer identity?

The queer community has not waited for the church to figure that out; it has provided its own answer in the language and practice of "family of choice," finding power in the idea that "family" does not denote a singular configuration. Even as we (cisgender, straight clergy and the churches we serve) adjust our lenses to recognize nuclear families of a thousand, thousand varieties, the LGBTQ+ imagination goes beyond the householding arrangement to locate and identify the family of choice much more broadly—in the club, at the gym, on the protest/parade circuit, and in many more places outside the domestic kitchen-and-living-room setting that is traditionally the theater for family interaction.

Family-of-choice language has been a gift to my church, cracking open the insular and exclusive familial language of small, conserving congregational life. Contemporary congregations had already been warned about crowing happily that "We're all family here!" After all, it's nearly impossible to become part of a family you weren't born into, right? But still we use that family language in the church, and not only because it runs through the Bible. We want to say that we're tight with each other, that we are sharing life together, not just enjoying the privileges of membership à la church-as-club. "Hey, fam, what's good?" a person (less than) half my age called out before worship a few years ago, and I've taken that language as my own, in spite of being uneasily aware that newcomers among us might not feel included.

But the family of choice always makes room at the table for newcomers in need of companionship. By definition, no one is born into the family of choice; we all chose to be here of our own accord, born again in our baptisms, and thus members of a whole new family. That recognition spreads responsibility for relationship maintenance among all those who are *choosing* to be family for each other. To choose to be family is to have each other's backs, to love each other's emerging identities, to share resources without strings. It's more deliberate than the accident of birth that landed you in your family of origin.

Family-of-choice practice has helped us claim Jesus's promise that, despite the family-fracturing consequences of pursuing the gospel and all that it means for our life, there is a new family waiting for us in the church:

> Jesus said, "Truly I tell you, there is no one who has left house or brothers or sisters or mother or father or children or fields, for my sake and for the sake of the good news, who will not receive a hundredfold now in this age—houses, brothers and sisters, mothers and children, and fields, with persecutions— and in the age to come eternal life." (Mark 10:29–30)

I used to worry that Jesus was writing checks his church couldn't cash. Were we really ready to stand in the gaps left by hard-hearted families of origin? (On a practical level, how many times would we help a gig-economy worker move from one crappy apartment to another?) The closer I came to queerly beloved families of choice, and the more I was encouraged to imagine our church as a family of choice, the more eagerly I embraced Jesus's certainty that we could do it.

But.

There remains the painful reality that people are biologically, subconsciously, emotionally, and spiritually hungry for the love and affection of their families of origin. They are the people who brought you into the world and kept you alive when you couldn't, the people who remember things about your childhood that you don't, the people who watched you grow and helped or hindered your becoming in countless ways, the people whose DNA and in-jokes and accent and history you inherited. These are the people who, out of all the people in the whole wide world, should love you best because they loved you first. And when they don't, the well of pain never runs dry, no matter how secure your family of choice.

And now here you are in my office, asking me what to do: whether to try again to be in relationship with the ones who have let you down, and if so, how; or whether it might be okay to cut them loose, wash your hands of it all, and forever grit your teeth through that one part of the Lord's Prayer: "Forgive us . . . as we forgive those who have sinned against us." What does that forgiveness require of us, practically speaking? Do I have to go home for Thanksgiving if they use my dead-name, try to set me up on straight dates, make my spouse and me sleep in separate rooms?

The Gift of Testimony and the Gift of Listening

To all the brave and beautiful souls who are working through this anguish I want to say, *we* (the cisgender-normative, heteronormative church and its clergy) are the ones who should be asking *you*. I have come to understand that LGBTQ+ persons who have held on to their Christian faith after all the shit the cis-het-normative church has put them through belong in the rarified category *True Believers*. I've come to believe that the Spirit of the living Christ resides especially deeply in those who have been told repeatedly that their identity is a tragic mistake, something significantly less than the *imago Dei* enjoyed by cisgender/straight people, *and who still believe that God walks with them every day of the world.*

I've heard powerful, inspiring, and heartbreaking stories from queer beloveds about their relationships with their families of origin. I've witnessed the tenderheartedness of some who forgive the close-mindedness of their relatives again and again with no loss of dignity, hiking the arduous high road that makes them stronger day by day. I also believe those who tell me it was necessary to excise toxic relationships from their lives in pursuit of mental health, the deserved wholeness that God intends for their being. I am amazed at the creativity of some who find complex workarounds for spending time with their families of origin, and I'm aware of the care that their emotional and spiritual exhaustion will require after a season spent on that high wire.

Storytelling in the Image of God

Indulge me for a minute while I tell you why I think this is so critically important, beginning with the dreaded words, "Let me tell you about my doctoral work. . . ." Some years ago I completed a Doctorate of Ministry project that required me to dip my toes into the deep waters of narrative theory. My wholly amateur understanding of it, as it relates to Christian theology and human existence, goes like this. God ordered the world in such a way that all creation experiences linear time flowing in one direction toward the future. But we humans have a reflective capacity, an ability to look backward along our experience of time; and uniquely among all the creatures God has made, we narrate our past experience to make sense of it. We string together the moments of episodic existence by telling sense-making stories of ourselves in the world. This is meaning-making; this is identity formation; this is how we know who we are.

Moreover, it's one of the ways we are made in *imago Dei*, in God's image, because God is the Prime Storyteller, teaching us how to be in relationship with God and with each other and with creation by telling stories about all of us together (a.k.a. the Bible, a unified story of God and God's world). Jesus took after his Parent in Heaven, stitching together the reign of God he came to show us with parables, jokes, riddles, and "once upon a times." The early church followed his lead, communicating the identity of Jesus for the sake of generations to come by telling stories about him: what he did, what he said, what he suffered.

I believe that if the Spirit of the risen Christ inhabits and empowers the church today, then one of the things it's making possible and necessary for us is our own narration of God-with-Us, God-in-the-World-God-Still-Loves. The church is (or ought to be) a storytelling lab, a rehearsal space for practicing our narrations of ourselves and each other as part of God's all-encompassing Story of Everything.

This idea finds its way into congregational practice when we make space and time for everyone's voice to be heard. Gilead Chicago, a new (b. 2015) church for spiritual refugees, embraces the credo "True stories save lives." Gilead invites worshipers to tell their own (prepared and practiced, but so real, so raw) stories around broad topics to the whole church as a part of worship—after which the pastor intones, "The word of God for the people of God!" and the congregation responds, "Thanks be to God!"

At Galileo Church, we begin every Sunday worship service with a query. "A query is an old question that people of faith have been asking each other for a long time," we say; we rotate through a set of familiar, contemplative questions every four weeks, giving everyone two minutes to answer out loud with a neighbor, if they like, or to meditate quietly on their own. The queries invite each person to assess their own spiritual health and flourishing, review the week just past, and articulate "how goeth it with thy soul" in the company of beloved community. We each tell little stories, strings of moments out of which we are learning to make sense. Because we practice, we get better at it. Many are the worshipers who have kvetched about queries when they first came to Galileo; many are the worshipers who now say their day-to-day lives are invested with meaning as they seek out answers to next Sunday's query well ahead of time.

Here is my point as it relates to LGBTQ+ Christians and their families of origin: these beloveds don't need a set of abstract instructions from a clergyperson (or anyone else) about how to love each other. Rather, the church could benefit greatly from LGBTQ+ Christians telling their own stories about what love (or the failure of love, as a sad but useful counterexample) looks like in their lives. What if, I started to wonder, we could create some space and time for these stories, thoughtfully and truthfully told by the people who lived them, as a way for all of us to learn better how to do the difficult work of loving across difference? It's a capacity that Christian life increasingly requires, because wide varieties of human identity and experience are increasingly present in our churches, our neighborhoods, and yes, our own families. (Thanks be to God.)

The Christian Practice of Testimony

It's not as if I invented the idea that Christians could learn from each other's stories. The Christian practice of *testimony* is as old as our ancestors in faith. There's the hilarity of the VRPs (Very

Religious Persons) pressing the formerly blind man to indict Jesus for his healing in John 9, the man repeatedly insisting, "All I know is, I was blind but now I see! I can't tell you what the guy looked like because . . . I was blind, see?" It's inarguable, because they're his eyes, and it's his healing. He asserts nothing except what has happened to him, his own irrefutable experience.

There's the lovely simplicity of Mary Magdalene returning from the empty tomb that first Easter day, not with an argument for resurrection or with an assertion of resurrection's meaning for the life of the world. She just tells what she's witnessed: "I have seen the Lord" (John 20:18). Mary M's straightforward subjectivity has inspired homileticians (see especially Anna Carter Florence and John McClure) to propose that more Christian preaching should be like that: a subjective confession of what the preacher has seen, from her own subjective experience of God's presence in the text and in the world.

But testimony is not only for preachers. Tom Long's *Testimony: Talking Ourselves into Being Christian* (Jossey-Bass, 2004, in The Practices of Faith series) proposes that the polite privatization of God-talk has robbed Christians of clarity of belief. You can't believe what you can't articulate, Long says, so the recovery and practice of talking with each other about our experiences of God and self are vital to the deepening of Christian faith.

Amanda Hontz Drury, in her book *Saying Is Believing: The Necessity of Testimony in Adolescent Spiritual Development* (IVP Academic, 2015), draws on her own experiences as a child and adolescent in congregations with a vibrant weekly practice of spontaneous, soulful testimony from individual worshipers to the whole church. As a youth minister, Drury came to understand that "narrative does more than *describe*; it also *constructs.* . . . [I]dentity is further developed when one's narrative is articulated" (25). She argues convincingly that the regular Christian practice of testimony—an expectation that any Christian should be able and allowed to tell the story of how God has been present, how their own life makes sense as part of God's story of the world—is an essential component of raising faithful kids into faithful adulthood. *Telling their story Christianly makes them Christian*, Drury might say.

So when an LGBTQ+ beloved tells me the story of their family of origin's acceptance or rejection, and usually a swirl of both, or when they tell me about the secrecy and fear, the revelation and relief, the shock and sorrow, the separation and reconciliation, the forgiveness and embrace, any combination of experiences that have gotten them *here*, to this place of good-enough shalom (about which I'll say more)—I'm saying that's testimony, and I'm saying that's Christian formation in action. I believe that the wide range of Christian LGBTQ+ people's responses to a family of origin's "less than love" (a.k.a. "I love you, but . . ." syndrome) *is Christian*, fundamentally, because *all* followers of Jesus are in a constant state of wrestling with the right/best/least-worst way to love our neighbors as we love ourselves, even when, especially when, they don't love us back. *That we are wrestling with it* is itself Christian, I'm saying.

Actually, it's not me saying it. It's all the aforementioned brave and beautiful souls who have sat with me and poured out their heartache over their families of origin, as well as all the ones who have no need of conversation with me to work it out, who are saying it. I want to share their stories with you so you'll have the same testimony, in hopes that perhaps you'll share it with whoever needs to hear it next.

The Christian Practice of Listening

Of course, all this narration of the self's subjective experience would be an intolerably narcissistic exercise if it were not offered for others' sake, in others' hearing. Thus, the church that learns to testify must also learn to listen, and likewise listening is an act of love. (There's a StoryCorps collection, *Listening Is an Act of Love* by Dave Isay [Penguin, 2007], that I love for the title as much as for the stories it contains.)

To collect stories from our LGBTQ+ beloveds and their families, I approached a gold-medal champion of the practice of listening, Galileo Church co-conspirator Susan Chiasson. Susan is a social scientist who is infinitely interested in the "why" of human beings. She is also a long-time friend with whom I have to carefully ration get-togethers because we will apparently never, ever run out of talk that pleases us both. As a conversation partner, Susan is smart and funny. She's always just read something that she knows I'll find fascinating; she's always curious about what I've been thinking about lately. She's a generous listener, even in her private life.

In her vocation as an interviewer, Susan has a way of gently probing, peeling back layers with excellent care until the interviewee's vulnerability bursts through in a shimmering show of rainbow-colored light—and not just for LGBTQ+ people. Her ways of asking and listening are indeed acts of love.

Transcripts of the long-form interviews Susan conducted over many months in 2018 and 2019 illuminated more complexities around how queer people navigate their families of origin than Susan and I had imagined. The transcripts came to me as Susan completed them, and while we got together once in a while to discuss the shape of this project, we talked surprisingly little about the details of the stories we had received from our friends. I believe we both intended, by unspoken agreement, to *listen to* our friends more than we *talked about* them, to let these narratives sink into our bodies and souls without too much chatter from two cisgender, straight people cluttering up the airwaves.

But finally, it was time to shape raw transcripts into something more shareable so that more people could join us in this sacred listening. I have done the regrettable work of drastically cutting down the transcripts of Susan's conversations in order to spotlight the themes that are most directly applicable to our one big question, "What's your relationship with your family of origin like?" Interviews became stories as Susan's questions dropped out and our friends' first-person narrations took shape. I took special care to preserve the voice and tone of each person's story, hearing my friends in my head as I worked. (And I'll go ahead and tell you, in the interest of transparency, that my first, second, and often third engagements with each transcript resulted in my being overwhelmed and in tears, my gratitude and awe spilling over as I read and listened.) While there's been some editing of sentences or phrases for clarity, the words belong entirely to the beloveds who opened their hearts to Susan. And then to me. And now also to you.

The Shape of Your Shalom

The call for interviews was not an open invitation within Galileo Church. Susan and I each remembered times that we'd sat with particular people, listening to their stories of coming out and all that came after, thinking, "Wow, this person has really done a lot of work to process all of this. So much drama, so much trauma, but this person is standing tall, clear-eyed, and stout of heart. That's pretty amazing." So we sought out people with whom we'd had that experience, people we felt had reached a kind of equilibrium with respect to their queer identity and their relationships with their families of origin. We hoped they could tell us how they got there.

We realized quickly, however, that "there" is different for different people. We would not be able to compile a bunch of stories that ended "happily ever after," not if we predefined "happily ever after" in any particular way. We needed people to tell us not just *how* they got there, but *where* they got to. We needed to know, "What is the shape of your shalom?" where *shalom* is an open category, ready to be defined by the one to whom it belongs.

Shalom is borrowed language, obviously. I'm a Western Christian borrowing it from my spiritual, if not literal, ancestors in faith, because my own language doesn't provide a singular word for such a fulsome concept. If I were to speak of "peace" instead, I might promote the mistaken assumption that the only destination these stories will honor is one where all conflict has been resolved and all parties are content, that is, living "happily ever after."

Shalom is used so variously by biblical characters and writers that it provides rich possibilities for describing the many ways our LGBTQ+ friends relate to their families of origin. For example, in the Bible shalom might refer to safety in travel, a freedom from fear of physical violence along the way. A major theme in our queer beloveds' coming-out stories is safety, as you'll see. Shalom can refer to a sense of satisfaction in a life well lived, so that one dies at peace. The narrators we're listening to have indeed "come to terms" (Susan's phrase, from her concluding essay) with their queerness and are at peace with what it means for their family relationships.

In biblical usage, shalom can also be political, as when an end to conflict has been negotiated. It doesn't mean everybody gets everything they want. It just means that the war is over. No more carnage. As a result of the cessation of hostilities, there are new possibilities for relationship. Not all of those possibilities will be realized, but at least they aren't preempted by violence. Many of our beloveds describe that kind of familial shalom—a treaty, an exhalation, a reprieve, a rest. Many have found themselves bending, becoming flexible toward their family members, for the sake of the imperfect relationship they have now, in hope of the better relationship that may yet flourish in seasons to come.

The highest conceptual usage of shalom that I understand is eschatological—the prophetic declaration that God has in mind not only the cosmic cessation of conflict but also the health and flourishing of the whole, interrelated creation, the repair of every broken piece of peace. Shalom in the fullest requires reconciliation in every fractured relationship—between humans and God, between humans and each other, between humans and the very ground of which we are made—because the well-being of every individual requires the well-being of all, the way God sees it. Imagine that.

When we children of Abraham, Sarah, and Hagar greet each with *Shalom*, or *As-salamu alaykum*, or *Peace of Christ*, we are leaning toward that eschatological, cosmic shalom. And we are admitting that, in the here and now, we get, at most, little glimpses of that shalom, enough to whet our appetites for God getting more of what God wants.

So Susan and I were not looking for LGBTQ+ persons with *ideal* relationships with their families of origin. (Why would we hold them to a far higher standard than any family of origin could truthfully boast?) We were simply looking for people and families on the other side of the fear and danger, the worry and regret, the conflict and violence, around queer identity and coming out. We were looking for the shape of each one's "good enough shalom"— the right-here-right-now sign of things to come when all God's dreams for all God's children come true. "What does it look like where you are?" became the gist of Susan's questions. And after that, "Can you tell us how you got there?"

WE'RE LISTENING

The Social Scientist's Introduction

Susan A. Chiasson (she/her)

When Katie approached me about this project, I said yes right away for a number of reasons. I wanted to give many of the queer people at Galileo Church—people I know, respect, and love—a safe way to tell their stories publicly. I believed that I, and others who listened to the stories of their lived experience, would learn something new about what Katie calls the "complexities around how queer people navigate their families of origin." I knew from past experience with Katie that talking to her about this project would add to my own spiritual education, and I liked the idea of combining our two perspectives, hers as a pastor and mine as a social scientist.

Katie and I began by identifying the people at Galileo who we believed had achieved peace with their families of origin or had at least reached a point of equilibrium acceptable to themselves. Then I invited them to talk with me. Over fifteen months I talked with fifteen people, a mix of younger and older, cis-het and queer, kids and parents, single and partnered, and we thought, *That's enough for us; we can't be exhaustive nor can we exhaust the goodwill of our community.* It's a big ask, what we were asking. We're grateful to the people who talked with us, grateful to those who considered but weren't able to do it, and grateful to Galileo Church for having a deep reservoir of kind, courageous, talkative, queer beloveds.

Our invitation made clear both the topic and our ultimate hope of publishing a book containing these narratives. I explained my credentials to our invitees: I'm a social science researcher who conducts interviews and focus groups on social and political issues for my day job (which means I do applied, not academic, social science). I have a beloved younger brother who came out decades ago and for whom I have rooted ever since. I'm a co-conspirator of Galileo Church. All of which means, I told them, I'm professionally and personally invested in not screwing this up.

To that end (not screwing up), I proceeded carefully. I conducted the interviews in private settings where we wouldn't be interrupted or overheard. Our interviewees understood that the conversations were recorded and would be transcribed and that they could refuse to answer any question or terminate the conversation if they weren't comfortable. (No one did, I'm happy to report.) They were assured of confidentiality and anonymity. I explained that transcripts of their interviews would go next to Katie for shaping into first-person narratives in the interviewees' own voices and that they would get to review their stories and consent to their publication.

For any social scientists reading this, you should know that our exploration of this topic doesn't follow academic guidelines about sampling and saturation points (where you talk to enough people that you start hearing the same ideas repeated again and again). In terms of ethics, we made sure people knew what would happen, secured their consent, and let them know they could come back to us with concerns. Our approach combines practical pastoral concerns (about which Katie has more to say) and grounded theory (that's my part). Grounded theory begins with a person's everyday experience and uses that to reach an understanding of a social phenomenon. It's inductive, from the ground up, with no big data sets, statistics, or predictions. For Katie and me, understanding comes from listening to people answer very simple questions about their experience and then reflecting carefully and respectfully on their answers.

I've found that having a few main questions keeps an interview on track but allows wiggle room for the occasional digression. Here, I asked

- What was it like for you, coming out to your family of origin and your extended family of origin?
- What were the reactions of members of your family of origin and how did you handle them?
- How are you today with those family members?
- What role, if any, did church play in this process?
- What compassionate and practical advice would you give to your younger self?

I also showed each person a collection of photographs on small cards to begin the interview and at various points along the way. I instructed each person, "Choose a picture that captures what coming out was like for you. You have ten seconds. Trust your hands." Each time, I was struck by how quickly people selected a card and how easily they could describe their overall experience based on that visual image. I took photos of their selections so Katie and I could look at them as we went over transcripts later. The pictures and the questions generated a rush of words. Our transcripts are 95 percent interviewee stories and 5 percent me asking a question or saying, "Hmmm," "Uh-huh," and "Can you say more?"

I hesitated to ask one question: *Do you wish all of this had never happened?* It seemed harsh, as though I were trying to use a counterfactual question to erase identity and experience. In the first interview, I didn't ask it. But when I asked the interviewee my standard clean-up question ("Is there something I should have asked you and didn't?"), he said, "You should have asked if I was sorry this happened." So I asked right then and there and in every interview after that. While some wished that the *how* of coming out had played out differently, only one wished that it had not happened (and what that person really wished was that society had been kinder to them about the possibility of marrying and having kids).

People don't choose to be queer or to be related to queer people, but they can choose how to come to terms with queerness. These friends told us, bravely and honestly and thoughtfully, why they came out to their family of origin and what it was like to do that. A number of them also told us why they agreed to talk to us about something so personal. Evelyn sums it up: *I would do anything to help any young person—or old person—coming out. It's like, this is it. This is the shit. You know? It's the truth.* Or, as Katie might say, *This is my testimony.*

To which we were honored to respond, *Go ahead. We're listening.*

· THE STORIES ·

ALL OF ME

Jake (he/him)

Jake (he/him) is in his mid-thirties. He is studying theology in graduate school in preparation for Christian ministry in a setting yet to be determined but with the aim of helping LGBTQ+ Christians who have been traumatized by the church.

Jake describes a long trajectory of coming to terms with his dual identity as gay and Christian in a family, a church, and a world that believe you can be one or the other, but not both. From age thirteen to age thirty, he studied and prayed. He submitted to conversion therapy in hopes of marrying a woman and having a fruitful career in Christian ministry. After persevering for months, he at last concluded such therapy was "bullshit."

Now Jake refuses to choose between his sexual orientation and his faith, describing his spiritual practice as "defiant." But he feels lonely when he's with his family—lonely because they cannot accept him as both/and, wishing instead for the uncomplicated Jake of their childhood together.

I HAVE A BIG FAMILY: six younger siblings and my dad. I had to come out multiple times. I tried to orchestrate it so that I could come out to all of them all at once, but that did not work. Instead I had to come out to every single one of them separately.

Once we got together for a family birthday party or something, and my whole family was actually there. We don't even all get together for Christmas anymore because we just live in so many different places. But this time everyone was there. It was afternoon; we were all just relaxing. I'm like, *This would be a perfect time!* But also, *It's a birthday and I don't want to ruin it. I don't know how everyone's going to react.* Trying to manage seven other people's emotions with me coming out just seemed like it would be chaos. So I gave up on it. I ended up coming out over seven months. I was thirty years old.

My brother was the last one I came out to. And that was the hardest one, because he was my closest friend, and he's the most theologically conservative person in my family. He tried to tell me all these reasons why his view was correct and mine was not. Our relationship has never really recovered. On one hand, I realize that it's not my fault. But on the other hand, I'm the person who got him involved in the church in the first place. So I feel some responsibility for what became of our friendship because of that.

The first person I came out to was my youngest sister. She was a safe person to test this out on. She was like, "I think you're wrong, but I also know that you've really studied this and you've prayed about it, so I'm just going to trust that you know what you're doing." My relationship with her has been confusing. Last fall I thought she had finally come to fully accept me. And then we had a conversation where it turns out that she still thinks same-sex relationships are wrong. And then for Christmas, she bought me a pride flag. I don't understand. I'm very confused.

My other four sisters have more or less reached the point where they just don't talk about it. Last Christmas, we were home and playing games, and one of the questions was, "Who do you think the hottest celebrity is?" My brother wasn't there. We were all talking about guy celebrities. And none of them had any issue with it, with me finding guys hot. But at the same time, they aren't interested in knowing more about my romantic life. Honestly, I think that's awkward for my whole family, because my whole family is weird with romance. They just don't know how to talk about it. We don't have any established protocol in the family, so I think they don't know what to do.

As for my dad, I was really nervous telling him. He's a committed Republican, but he's also libertarian. So we had this long conversation. And I just kept not actually saying it. After an hour of talking, I worked up the courage to finally say that I was gay. He was like, "Okay, so?" He was of the mind that I have to do what I have to do. He hasn't made an effort to understand the gay community, or LGBT rights, or the politics of that. But multiple times, he's asked if I'm dating anyone. Or he'll say, "You should check out those Log Cabin Republicans. They're all gay." And I'm like, "Dad, that is not going to work out."

As for my mom, she passed away in 2007, so I never came out to her. When I was thirteen, shortly after I figured out I was gay, one of my siblings asked my mom what "gay" was. That was the year Ellen [DeGeneres] came out. My mom gave us this long lecture about what homosexuality was. She said that it was a mental illness. At that point I resolved that I wasn't going to tell anybody. It never crossed my mind that I would ever come out to my mom.

My parents considered themselves Christian, but me and my siblings grew up with this belief that God is good and Christians are bad. Christianity was not a defining part of my upbringing. I didn't go to church until I was twenty-six. It's weird, but I knew I was gay before I started coming to church. I brought a lot of my siblings with me. We had this common faith as young adults that we didn't have growing up.

Because of my faith, I so desperately needed to be straight. I went into denial for a long time. I convinced myself that I actually was straight. But all of the mental gymnastics my brain had to do to convince myself of that—it was exhausting. I entered a really deep depression, ended up suicidal.

The only other gay Christian I had ever known was this really sweet guy named Michael, who was gay and Catholic. He eventually walked away from the church because they could not accept his sexuality. And I said, "I don't want to leave the church. I don't want to leave God and Jesus. But I don't know how I can continue to be gay, because nobody's going to accept me." I ended up coming out to a pastor I had worked for, who said I couldn't work in ministry anymore because I was gay. He told me that eventually I was going to have to choose: Jesus or being gay.

But I kept feeling like this is who God made me to be. I got to this point where I couldn't say that I was following God and *not* come out—which was the most terrifying realization I've ever come to. Because that meant I would have to start telling more people. I started telling most of my family. I started telling my friends. I started telling the people I'd worked for. I started very slowly making gay posts on Facebook. And sharing things from LGBT organizations. Hinting at it.

I have a half-brother, eight years older than me. Our family's relationship with him is complicated. But he noticed what I was doing on Facebook and messaged me. I'm like, "Oh shit." He was vocally anti-Christian. I was less worried about coming out as gay to him, and more worried about admitting that I was still a Christian. So we Skyped, and we talked about it. I told him that I was gay, and he said that he and his wife were in my corner 100 percent. He said that if things got dicey with the family, or with the church, or if I just didn't feel safe in Idaho, that I could come out and stay with them if I needed to. Which was greatly reassuring, even if they weren't really okay with me being Christian.

A few weeks ago, I shared about my half-brother in the communion meditation at our church. The church posted my words online, and I sent my half-brother the link. He told me, "I wish that there were more people of faith like you. I wish there were more people who led with love. The world needs more Christians like you." That was one of the most moving things anyone had ever told me. He is the first family member I have who understands both parts of me—

gay and Christian—even though he's not gay, and he's not Christian. The rest of my family, they don't understand me at all, how the two parts fit together. They don't really want to know me.

My younger brother, he doesn't think I'm following Jesus. So he doesn't really care about my life because he thinks I walked away from God. Never mind that I'm going to seminary! That I regularly attend church! That I'm part of the church leadership, even. I'm all in! And he's still like, "No."

Last December I went home for two weeks, thinking that yeah, it would be nice to see my family, to hang out, because I'm not going to see them again for probably another year. And it was just the longest two weeks. I felt the whole time like I had to be this other person for them, this other version of Jake that they feel they've always known. It was hard and exhausting, because I couldn't really be me. It is so lonely, not having that family.

When I'm in good mental health, I get through it by saying, "This has been lonely, but they're better than they were." So there's hope that they'll be better still in the future. And the times when I'm not as healthy, it feels like I just fucked it all up. Like, if I had just been better, and by that I mean, if I'd just been straight, things would be fine. I would have a great relationship with my younger brother, because I would be who he expected me to be. None of my siblings would be awkward around me. I'd have a family.

But here's the thing. I've thought about this a lot. I am 90 percent certain that if I was straight, I would not be a Christian right now. The only reason that I spent so much time in prayer, and reading the Bible, and working through all of these faith things is because I needed to know what God thought about me. I needed to know if God accepted me as I was or if I needed to change. I invested countless hours in prayer. I fasted once for an entire month, like Jacob wrestling with God. I said, "I am not going to give up until you give me the blessing. Until you tell me one way or the other."

And I had this revelation that God fully accepted me for being gay. The one thing that holds me to my faith is that I'm queer. This is how I connect with God. Because we have a very queer God, and I'm a very queer man. My queerness, in the image of God, is what gives me my faith. If I lose my queerness, what kind of faith is left?

That's something my family is never going to see, I don't think. Even if my older brother fully supports me and understands where I'm coming from, he doesn't really know the finer points of my faith. And if I were to tell him, "My queerness is the image of God," he would be like, "Oh sure, okay, whatever works." But he wouldn't get it.

And in the same way, the rest of my family will never be able to grasp that this thing that has been so foundational to my faith, this image of God in me, is also this controversial thing. My family would just look at me and think, "Sure, Jake, whatever you say."

Something that people never tell you is that coming out is a continual process. That it never stops. That even if you're Ellen DeGeneres, not everyone knows that you're gay. And I talk to other Christians about being queer. I was able to cultivate enough respect in my friendships before I came out that people still extended that to me afterwards. They would be like, "But this is Jake. We know him." I won't say it necessarily shifted people all the way over to affirming. But they're not antigay anymore, which honestly, I will take.

It can be very easy for LGBT Christians to let go of faith, because other Christians don't trust that we have it. But I'm not giving them that power. I pray a lot of times just out of pure defiance. I pray for all the people who said that I would not be able to hold onto my faith after I came out.

IN MY OWN HEAD

Cole (he/him)

Cole (he/him) is in his early thirties. He works as a barista and is taking college courses toward a counseling degree. He describes a family of origin that was (mostly) ready to accept his identity as a gay man long before he was.

The relief that came from finally articulating what everybody knew opened Cole's relationships with his family members. It's not perfect—extended family members are still insensitive and stubbornly fundamentalist in their reading of Christian scripture—but Cole knows he's supported by the people who matter most to him.

Despite a recent divorce from his husband of seven years, Cole feels hopeful about his future. He has returned to church after many years of (deserved) distrust of the institution and is returning to his ancestral roots to help his affirming grandparents on their farm.

MY STORY IS, I started coming out . . . and then I went back in. And then I came out again.

I was fifteen or sixteen the first time. On TV they interviewed a guy who was an underwear model. I made a mental note of that, and later, on our family computer, I looked up images of that guy in his underwear. My dad later saw what I had been looking at. My parents sat me down and said, "Hey, we saw these images that you looked up. What's going on? Why did you search that?" It was really awkward.

I said, "Maybe I'm bisexual. I don't know what I am." My parents wanted to help me navigate this, so we made a plan of action. Step one: find a Christian counselor to help talk me through these feelings.

With that counselor, it was very much a "pray the gay away" thing. I started trying to focus our conversations on my depression rather than my sexuality. As soon as he would talk about something gay, I would say, "Oh, yeah, I know that's wrong." I would try to appease him so we wouldn't talk about it anymore.

I was going to a church youth group on Wednesday nights. I told the counselor about the youth group, and the next week, the youth pastor gave a sermon about gay being against the Bible. Nobody knew it was about me—except me. The kids were like, "Why are you even talking about this?" The youth minister said, "I know that somebody here is dealing with this."

I never confronted that counselor about what he did. But the older I get, I know that the counselor reached out to that youth minister and told him about me. It really messed up my relationship with the church. I felt like I couldn't trust, really trust, leaders in the church.

My parents were 100 percent unaware of that betrayal. They were like, "Okay, our son is really sad. We're going to let him figure this out." They wanted me to know it's okay, that being gay is fine. I heard them saying those things, but I wasn't ready to deal with my own identity in that way. I hadn't figured it out. It was more about me accepting myself. I don't think there was ever a fear of my family disowning me, but it was maybe a fear of, *How will this change everything?*

My family's really critical of people, whether they're straight or gay. I had a heightened sense of how critical they were about gay guys on TV, like Jack from *Will & Grace* or Carson on *Queer Eye for the Straight Guy*. Now I can see that they are equally critical about everybody. They were just being sarcastic, and I took it on.

But then I had this constant internal dialog: "I don't want to be like that. Maybe I *can* pray this away. Maybe if I focus, I won't have to be gay like those guys."

So I regressed. I went back in the closet. I told my parents, "I'm straight, I'm straight." They said, "Okay." I dated my sister's best friend, which felt safe because I had known her for a long time. I've talked to my dad about all this and he said, "Well, we all knew that you were gay. We knew that you were giving it your last college try, trying to be straight for yourself or for us. But we knew you had to figure it out for yourself."

I wish I would have known then that everything was going to be fine. But we were still attending a church that said that it was wrong, and my parents were sending me to a counselor who kept trying to change me. So I thought that's the way my parents wanted me to handle this.

After a long time, I came to a point in my own life where I was content with who I was. I was even happy. I had a great network of friends. "Born This Way" [by Lady Gaga] had just come out. It was like this bubble burst. I was finally, like, "It's okay to be gay!" I was twenty-three or twenty-four at this time.

I talked to close friends first. I had a really great network of friends. I talked to one of them and asked for advice. Then I wanted to tell my sister because I knew that she had spoken up for a lot of her friends that were gay. I tried to tell her one time, but I chickened out. I kept waiting for her to ask me, "How's your life? What's going on?" I kept waiting for anyone, at that point when I was ready to tell people, to ask me, "What's new?" But nobody was asking me that.

Another time, driving my sister home, I thought, "I'm just going to tell her." I remember crying in the car and she said, "I love you." And I said, "I love you, too." It was really great.

A few days later, I had dinner with my mom at a taco restaurant and I told her. She actually asked. She was sensing everything happening, and she guessed: "So, Cole, do you want to be with men?"

I was so ready to tell her. I got emotional again. She asked, "Do you want to tell your dad tonight?" I said, "I'm so drained, I don't think I can tell him tonight. I do want to tell him. I just don't want to do it right now." And she's like, "I get it. I get it. But he's your dad and he's going to ask how tonight was. I'm going to probably tell him." I told her, "That's okay, you can tell him."

My dad is politically active in the Libertarian party. When I was twenty-one or twenty-two, he created a Libertarian party float for the gay pride parade. He built an Alamo that said, "Remember Stonewall" or something like that. My dad was in a gay pride parade before I was even out! So I came out to him over lunch and he talked a lot about the Bible. He made arguments against some of the "clobber" verses just like I've heard lately at Galileo Church, about history and context.

I remember feeling, "Oh my gosh, I just jumped off a cliff, and I don't know what I'm going to land on, but I feel good, because I've got my family, and this will change my relationship with my family." All of a sudden, I was more honest with them and they saw into my heart.

My mom, my dad, my sister, my brother-in-law, and even my grandparents—those core people who were in my life on a very regular basis—are affirming and they love me. But I do have people like my aunts, and some cousins, that aren't so welcoming. There was some turmoil when my cousins and my aunt didn't go to Christmas at my grandma's a few years ago because I would be there with my spouse. I didn't even know that at the time. What made me felt really great about that is, I had so many people on my side that were fighting for me. I love that I didn't even know that was going on.

So coming out, for me, made things better with my family. They were so excited for me. They could sense that I was in this new place in life, I was this new Cole that was really confident and unafraid. For so long, there had been this earworm in my head that said, "This will change everything. Don't you like how things are going right now? Why would you screw that up?" I just didn't see it clearly. I just couldn't figure it out for myself.

I found out recently that my parents left a church when I was a kid because the pastor said, "If anybody is gay, I don't even want them in the church." After the service my dad said to my mom, "We're never coming back here again." I never knew that story. But it's cool to hear it in retrospect.

A year or two after I came out for real, I remember talking with my grandpa. I was unsure of what he would think because they're so religious. My grandpa said, "Do you know how many men came out to me when I was a preacher? Men who said, 'Please change this about me. I have this attraction that I can't turn off, please help me.'" He said the more he learned about the historical context of the Bible, the less he thought the Bible was against people like me. That was such a relief. I took a big breath after he said that. "Wow, you get it, Grandpa; and not only that, you're teaching me stuff I didn't know about the Bible."

With my extended family, avoidance is a big part of how we get along. My aunt, one year during the holidays, mentioned a verse in Romans or something, and I just had to . . . I don't know. It's just easier to. . . . It's a crowded room. It's easier to just shift the conversation, like, "Okay, well, A. [Cole's sister], tell me about what's going on with your life."

Sometimes on Facebook, an uncle might post stuff that sends me over the edge. I'll type out a response and then think, "Never mind." Before I hit the submit button, I think, "Are they going to come at me with even more of their bullshit? Am I equipped to deal with that bullshit?" Usually the answer is, "I don't have time for that." Online, it's just not worth it. I don't engage that way.

I always believed Jesus's message was, "I will love you no matter what, and I'm going to forgive you no matter what." But what I always wondered was, "Well, why is it wrong in the first place, this thing I can't even help? I'm not harming anybody." I struggled with that. I thought, "Okay, well, Jesus loves me, but does that mean I have to sacrifice being a sexual person to walk with Jesus through my life? Does that mean I have to be single for the rest of my life?"

But I want to hold on to this faith. I'm still a spiritual person, but it felt like I had to give that up in order to be myself. When I came out, I didn't think about spiritual things for a long time. A lot of gay people I met out there, they had been hurt by the church. I still had a connection with God and faith, but not church.

Something I've really loved about Galileo Church is the intentional decisions that the church is making about how to communicate, "This is a safe place." When I met Galileo Church, I started thinking, "This is so progressive and so cool that they're doing things this way." I'm on this Galileo high right now. I'm just glad to be back in church.

And I'm actually looking forward to the future now. My grandparents are going through health issues. They have a farm, so I'm going to move in with them and help out. It's the LGBTQ affirming grandpa, which is kind of awesome.

So yeah, I'm happy that this happened. Being gay made me a stronger person. I had to be content with myself before I could share myself with anybody else. Yeah, I'm happy that it happened. And my relationship with my family is awesome.

A LIFELONG QUEST FOR UNCONDITIONAL LOVE

Evelyn (she/her)

E velyn (she/her) is in her mid-forties. She works as a nurse
in the psychiatric department of a public hospital. She has
been married to her wife for nine years, and together they
have three school-aged children.

Evelyn endured a childhood marred by chronic sexual
abuse by a family member, the disclosure of which led her parents to protect her appropriately from further harm. But as she
sought more than protection, finding true love with a teenage
girlfriend, the limitations of her parents' care were revealed.
Even as they came to accept her identity as a lesbian, they were
not well-practiced in freely expressing unconditional love.

To this day, Evelyn critically examines every relationship—
in her family, among her in-laws, within her church, in friendships mediated by social media—to find out, "Peel back the
layers, and what do you really feel about me?" In a familial
journey covering decades, she feels as if she finally has her parents' love. It doesn't stop her wishing it had not taken so long.

I CAME OUT WHEN I was fifteen years old. It was very dark. It was very,
very troubling. It was very rough. I felt like I was in a hole that
I couldn't get out of. Trapped.

I met a girl in high school who was my best friend, and it became an intimate relationship, and then we became girlfriends, and then we were like very closeted. We didn't even know what gay meant, really, being gay or lesbian.

My girlfriend came over on a weekend. We went to my room and shut the door. I don't remember if it had a lock, but my parents were upset. They brought me into their room and asked me if we had a relationship. I said yes. And the bottom kind of fell out.

My mother sobbed. My father said, "If we ever see her on this property again, we'll physically remove her." I remember seeing my mom kind of slouched on the bathroom floor just sobbing, sobbing, saying every time she thinks of us together it makes her want to vomit. My father told me I should go get a shotgun and blow their brains out because the pain would be easier to deal with.

All I could think of was the one being, the one person, that I loved and that loved me back, the one I had really, really, really felt love with. I mean, my parents always took good care of us, you know; we had everything we ever needed or wanted. But my mom was hard. She wasn't affectionate and my dad certainly wasn't.

I guess I was surprised that they didn't just love me for who I was. Like there were conditions attached to their love. I didn't feel like I was doing anything wrong. I wasn't a bad kid. I wasn't. I just didn't understand why being loved was so bad.

I ended up dropping out of high school and running away with an older woman because my parents weren't having me being a lesbian. She was probably in her forties. I did drugs with her. I did acid with her. I just had to escape, even though at the time I probably couldn't process that or think about that logically. All I knew was what felt good, and I had to get away from what felt bad. But my parents decided, once they couldn't find me—it was days they couldn't find where I was or who I was with, and they searched everywhere—they decided that nothing else mattered except getting me home. They realized that I wasn't gonna change and that I wasn't going to conform to being straight.

They were very loving: "We're sorry." My mom had found out that we ran away to Austin, and she told me she drove down there and drove up and down 6th Street, looking for me and just saying, "Nothing else matters." It was a turning point.

After that I just remember them letting me go. Right at eighteen, I just started doing my own thing and they had to accept it. All their friends were the upper crust, surgeons and doctors. I think they were embarrassed for quite a long time. They didn't know how to introduce me or how to talk about me. It took time, but it got easier and easier.

But I still remember, when I was a little girl, fifth or sixth grade, my mother bought me this pink sweatshirt, and it had white sheep all over the front, and one black sheep. I already felt like the outsider, the black sheep of the family, that they labeled me. And that has been the hardest thing, feeling like an outsider in my own family. Like their love was conditional.

One thing I didn't get from my mother a lot was hearing her say, "I love you." Or my dad. One thing I knew: I was always going to tell my kids how much I love them, always, even if it we're just in the car, you know. Even with my son, our teenager, if we're having issues, if we're having tough conversations, we always say, "We love you. This is why you need us. We love you and we just want you to know that we will always love you no matter what. No matter what."

My wife and I talk about that, what it would have been like for us, if we'd had that support in our families. What would it have been like to receive that, you know? For someone to say, "We love you no matter what." We don't know.

On my wife's side of the family, they're not okay with our relationship. I find myself not saying what I mean on social media, not saying what I want to say, not posting what I want to post. To protect, I don't know, maybe my wife, or maybe them. It bothers me. Like, why am I doing this? I'm hiding, I'm hiding, I'm hiding.

I censor myself but then I get pissed because I'm like, "This is my fucking page, I can put whatever I want on this page. It's mine. If they don't want to see it they can unfollow me."

But then I still don't do it, because of my wife's family, but also my own friends. How can I get 165 likes on something that doesn't matter at all, but then I post something about gay marriage and it's silent from every straight person I know? When you peel back those layers, how do they really feel about me? Do they really support my family? Am I self-censoring because I'm afraid I won't be loved unconditionally? Like when I was a child? I'm still afraid of that feeling.

I'm surprised at where I am today. I remember holding a gun in my hand . . . when all this was going on. I'm not sorry that all of this has happened, though. I feel like it's made me who I am today. I feel like I had to go there to get here. I wouldn't have had the experiences and the therapy and the books, the education, the self-help. When I graduated from nursing school, I wanted to be a labor-and-delivery nurse. But the manager of the psychiatric department called me and said, "I know you didn't apply for psych, but I have an opening. I'm wondering if you're willing to come interview for it?" I've been a psychiatric nurse ever since. It's where I'm supposed to be. Everything I went through got me here.

Obviously I still feel raw about a lot of things. I'm still very emotional about a lot of it, because it was very painful. I have been in therapy for a long time about a lot of it. But I would do anything to help any young person—or old person—coming out. It's like, this is it. This is the shit. You know? It's the truth. It's the shit.

DON'T ASK. DON'T TELL.

Marion (she/her)

Marion (she/her) is in her late fifties. She works as an elementary school educator who specializes in teaching kids with dyslexia to read and succeed in learning. She plays the upright bass in a small band.

Marion has been proactive about seeking community for her whole gay self, including relocating across several states in search of safe space to "just be." At the same time, she is deeply protective of her identity, exercising privacy to an extent that some would derisively call "closeted." For Marion, this is an exercise of care and respect for a family of origin she cherishes.

But from the beginning, Marion was open with the God she was sure always loved her. She has waited a long time for the people of God to catch up.

MY COMING-OUT STORY is that mostly I didn't. There was a lot of fear, so I was out only to the person I was in a relationship with, okay? Until the night of the marriage decision from the Supreme Court, June 26, 2015. I went to a celebration that night, and there I told a couple strangers. Not family.

I realized I was gay in 2003 when I fell in love with my best friend. I wasn't safe, wasn't safe anywhere, not at my work, not with my family, not anywhere. I don't know that I would have lost my job as a teacher, but nobody would have wanted their kid in my class had they known, and I would have been talked about terribly in the community. It would not have been accepted in the community where I taught at all. There were people who would just try to ruin you.

When I moved here [to Texas], my not-so-secret hopes were that I could make friends, I could find community, and I could meet people. I could meet somebody I could be in a relationship with. I had a couple of friends here, and they knew, so that was a start. My secret hope was that I would find a church.

The next people I told were Galileo Church people, at Pride in October 2015. The first person I talked to there was [Rev.] Katie [Hays], the very first person. I saw the Galileo float in the parade and it was like, "Yes! There's a church!" And as the Galileo folks went by, the backs of their t-shirts said, "We're not the center of the universe." Galileo, science, yes! After the parade I saw the Galileo booth that had a banner about "seeking spiritual refugees," and Katie was there, which was a good thing for me because she was close to my age.

I raised my hand, literally raised my hand, and said, "That's it! That's it! I'm a spiritual refugee!" But I was still a little pissed off at people, and I crossed my arms, I'm sure, and I said to Katie, "I just want to tell you, God and I are fine. God and I do not have a problem. But people and I are not okay. People and I are not okay." When I went to a Gay Christian Network conference a couple of years ago, there were all these books about "God loves me," meant to convince you that even though you're gay, God still loves you. What the hell? I don't need all those books. God and I were always fine. Anyway, Katie said, "I can't tell you how many people have said that to me." And we talked. I came to Galileo Church the next day.

So, about my family. I have also told R. [Marion's daughter], the younger of my two kids. I guess I needed a deadline, and she was coming to visit. She liked what I'd told her about Galileo, and she wanted to visit my church with me, so I knew I had to tell her. I felt like it would be a safe experience, partly because I'd seen how she acted with her friends who were gay. I'd seen her stand up to my daddy when he said something derogatory about one of her best friends who's a gay guy. But still, I'm her mama. Even though I knew that she has this in her, it was still very scary because I'm her mama, and that's just a different ball game.

Before she came here, I went to visit her at Christmas. We were watching something on Netflix and I paused the TV and said, "I need to tell you something. I'm gay." I was prepared for questions, but she asked none. I said, "I'm not in a relationship." She said, "Okay, but please tell me later on if you are. Tell me, I want to know."

I said, "I'm not telling J." That's my son. She looked up, she paused, and she said, "Yeah, I wouldn't tell J." I have never told him. I took her at her word, figured she knows her older brother probably better than I do. So R. is the only family member who knows.

My parents are still alive. Mama is eighty-one and Daddy will be eighty this year. Because I'm a scaredy-cat, the chickenshit way is okay for me. They're already kind of old and probably we can just ride this out and I'll never have to tell them. If it were somebody younger than me, that wouldn't be a wise thing for them to do. But age is kind of on my side. I might get away with it. My brother doesn't know, his wife, my niece and nephew, nope. People may suspect something, but it's never been confirmed. Don't ask, don't tell. That's the chickenshit way.

So that's usually my out, saying "that's the chickenshit way." It's a way for me to disarm somebody if they think in their mind, "Oh, that's chickenshit, keeping it secret." Because other people will say, "I can't live like that." So I just take away their power to judge me and say it for them. But for me, it's the thing I've chosen to do. It's the right thing for me at this moment. It's the right thing. And I wouldn't dare think that anybody else was chickenshit, whatever they did. So maybe it's not chickenshit for me, either.

If I told my parents, Mama'd probably cry, Daddy'd probably cry, I don't know. Mama would take to her bed. She would take to the couch and say, "I just don't know how to deal with it." I don't really hear Mama talking bad about people, but I've heard Daddy say things. I have heard Mama, more than once, if there's somebody in the community who's not married, usually a guy who's not married for a long, long time, she'll be talking to another lady in the church and she'll say, "Do you think he's . . . ?" and there's a pause, just dead space. "Do you think he's . . . ?" Well shit, I don't want them talking about me like that.

I've wondered what I'd do after, because shoot, they could live to be a hundred. But let's assume that they don't. If Mama and Daddy were gone, would I then tell my brother and my sister-in-law? I've wondered, and that's a possibility, but it would be later.

Also it's made much simpler because now I'm not in a relationship. What if I were in a relationship? Then it's a whole 'nother thing. I was in a relationship, but all they knew was that it was my best friend. That's what they knew.

I grew up in church. I was in church in my mother's womb. I sat through Mama's choir practices when I was a little bitty kid. But why did I stay in church after it had already become a place that I didn't fit? Community. There's that longing, for that sense of belonging in a community. I'd had it before. I knew what it felt like. Although I knew that in the past I had altered my own self, changed, conformed, to stay in it. I had conformed in the past, and I was good at conforming.

I would tell a young me that you didn't have to date those guys to be in the club. I dated guys in high school, like everybody did. I don't know what it means about me. All I know is that at these certain points in my life I went along, I was in the club. I went to school in a very small town. I graduated with sixty-four people. We started first grade together. We were in Sunday school together, and our mamas went to high school together. I wanted that community not to be messed up. So I conformed.

I'd probably also tell my younger self not to shut up at the dinner table. These days, I tend to keep things bottled up until it comes out like an explosion, because growing up you couldn't disagree with Daddy. He would say his piece, and then say, "There will be no discussion." I'd just put my head down, eat my food. I had lots of thoughts, and I thought I was going to choke on them.

Even now, I tend to just not say anything around my daddy. I don't want to get in an argument. So if my daddy says something racist or whatever, I just leave the room because I'm not going to change his mind. When I examine myself when I'm around my parents, I feel like I'm stuffing a lot. Mama has said, "Oh, be nice to Daddy, he's not well," in a shaky voice she doesn't normally have, but she almost cries and lays some guilt on me.

So I just don't say anything. I stay away from them. Now I get a hotel room when I visit them. Mama told me, after last time when Daddy was so mean, "We had a come-to-Jesus and he promises he's not going to be so ugly anymore." But now I get a hotel room. When I visit this summer do I get a hotel again? Or stay with them? I don't know the right answer.

I protect my parents. I never let them know things I did in high school, no. They will die not knowing the things I did. Before it was my being gay that I needed to protect them from, it was my marriage. My husband was abusive in many ways, and I didn't let them know. I didn't. They were shocked, *shocked* when we divorced. I should have let them know. Had they known all along, they might not have been so shocked when I finally did it.

If it were my kids, I would hope that they would tell me all along. I hope that I have made it so that they can tell me. The message to myself as a parent has been, "Okay, you want them to be able to tell you these things."

I also protected the person I was in a relationship with. She would not have wanted it known. I'm also not out at work. I'm not in a relationship now, so it just doesn't come up. I don't go, "Hey y'all, I'm gay," like an announcement. For people who are my age, a lot of us may still be secretive. In your core, in memory from way back, it's almost at the DNA-level to keep it private. I don't tell just everybody.

Since I have lived here, I've found several communities where I can just be. Galileo was the first. I say I have a few different little tribes of people. And that feels really good. A few weeks ago at Trinity Pride, all my communities collided. It was a beautiful swirl of color. This is how I feel now most of the time, that I have all the things that community is supposed to be. I have a family of choice at Galileo, and some other groups, and they all came together that day at Pride. I didn't even know where to hang out, so I kept moving my chair from one group to another. And so long as I stay here, as long as I stay physically in the places where I'm loved and accepted and I can just be, then I feel good.

HIDING FOR TOO LONG

Leanne (she/her)

Leanne (she/her) is in her fifties. She recently married Ava (she/her), whose story immediately follows this one. Leanne works as a diagnostician in the public school system.

Leanne describes loving church as a child. Going to church was an intergenerational event, woven into the fabric of her family life, even if her father was more religiously adherent than her mother. She grieves her loss of faith alongside her loss of time with her family of origin—the church's rejection of her identity robbing her of both. Hiding her sexual orientation was a waste of time, she reflects: "Everybody knew."

She wishes now she could have those years back, the years she spent in the closet, the years of hiding in plain sight—not only for her own sake but for the sake of younger family members with their eyes on her. She hopes to communicate, by inviting even her less-than-accepting family members to her wedding, that there's no shame inherent in her identity or anybody else's.

THE PROCESS OF COMING OUT has had several potholes. To this day, I am unclear about where to go with certain relationships within my family of origin. I struggle with whether it's important to maintain that relationship, and then I'm reminded of the sunny spots, like my sister, who has been totally accepting. She's a bright spot in the whole coming-out thing.

I was raised in a very conservative family. I wasn't allowed to watch television, so I didn't really know what gay was until I went to college. At band camp before school started, at my small college in south Alabama, we had a party in the band room. The first chair flute player said, "Tonight you're going to see things that a lot of you have never seen before. There will be boys that dance with boys and girls that dance with girls. There will be some boys that come dressed in women's clothes."

So we go to that party, and sure enough, there are people of the same sex dancing together, and it just clicked right there: that was me! I still didn't know what it was, but I quickly figured it out. That was how I was different.

I didn't come out to my family until my thirties. I was well hidden for a long time. My dad died in my second year of college, and my mom lived seven hours away, so she wasn't there to monitor what was going on. It's easy to hide when you're that far away from home.

But most of my family probably already knew. I lived with a woman and moved halfway across the continent with her for work, but I pretended like no one knew. And they went along with it.

In 1996, maybe, my partner at that time got a call from a hospital in LA. Her brother was HIV-positive and had suffered a psychiatric breakdown. Her family had no idea her brother was HIV-positive. It came out that he had AIDS-related dementia. He died by the end of the year.

I'm at my mom's house when I get the call from my partner, and the whole story comes out. I tell my mom what's happening, and she says, "Are you okay?" I said, "Yes, I don't have AIDS." She says, "Does S. [my partner] have AIDS?", and I said, "No, we don't have AIDS." She never says, "Are you a lesbian?", and I never said, "Yes, I'm a lesbian." She obviously understood that I was queer.

The next question out of her mouth was, "What did I do wrong?" I said, "You didn't do anything wrong. It's just the way I was born." She cried and was upset, but it sort of put things into perspective because she wasn't going to have a child who was going to die of AIDS, and S.'s family was going to face that.

I never talked with my siblings about it until, after twenty-one years, I left S. My sister finally asked me about it. I said, "I'm going to leave S. I'm going to buy my own house." My sister was like, "If you need anything, I'm here." S. was so in the closet. We bought a house together, and she wouldn't put my name on the deed because that's a public record. When I left, I said, "I'm done being that far in the closet," but of course I was fifty years old. I'd been hiding for fifty years—not very well because everybody knew. When I told my nephew I was gay, he goes, "Oh, I've known that for a long time."

You deny a whole part of yourself when you agree to never talk about it. You think that it'll be safe and you'll save your family relationships if you hide. If you don't force people who don't want to know about it to know about it, then you don't have to risk those family relationships. Because you know they're not going to accommodate you. You come out of that fundamentalist, evangelical background, and you just know. It's preached about from the pulpits. Or maybe it's just an assumption we make about our families. But if you've lived long enough, you've heard the stories of gay people who've come out to their evangelical family members and are kicked out of their houses.

I wish I wouldn't have hidden as long as I did, because you're not really hiding. Everyone knows you're gay. Your family knows you're gay. You're actually losing those relationships you're trying to save with your family, because you're distancing yourself from your family members. You're really damaging the relationships you want to save.

Some people are braver than me. I wasn't very brave. But now I am.

Ava and I recently got married. My sister and her husband and her children traveled here for the wedding. We sent invitations to my brother and his children, and we didn't even get an RSVP card back saying no. We got nothing. I didn't expect the kids to come because we planned a wedding in October and they all have small children in school. I had told my brother that, because he called me when they got the save-the-date card and said, "Congratulations." He started hemming and hawing then. He goes, "Why did you plan a wedding in October? Why didn't you get married in the summertime?" I said, "Because it's so hot. Have you been in Texas in the summertime?" So we didn't get any RSVP cards from them.

My sister tried to engage him about why they weren't coming to the wedding, but she couldn't get an answer. She finally just gave up. So my brother called my sister during the wedding ceremony! He called and said, "Where are you?" She goes, "Where do you think we are? At our sister's wedding," and then she gave the phone to her husband because she was so mad she couldn't talk.

My sister has become more of an ally because her son has come out as gay. He just turned eighteen. He came out last year. He might have come out sooner than last year, but last year is when I figured it out. He spent last Thanksgiving with Ava and me, and he would not talk about it. I said to myself, "You set a terrible example for him, and now he thinks he has to hide because you hid." That was part of my reasoning of not hiding anymore: I have to set a better example for him.

My brother's son is openly homophobic, which worries my sister. She has not told my brother about her son. I'm still wrestling with that. Like, am I going to just let it go? When do you grow so apart from someone that even though they're your brother, you have nothing in common with them anymore? Or they have values that you can no longer tolerate?

It makes me really sad to think about giving up on my brother because we don't have parents left anymore. It's just us. That's what I'm wrestling with now. It's been six weeks since the wedding and I haven't talked to him. I have a feeling they don't follow me on Facebook anymore because I'm so political on Facebook.

I don't have a relationship anymore at all with any of my cousins except the one who's a lesbian out in Seattle. My other cousins are openly hostile to gay people on Facebook. All you have to do is take one look at my Facebook page and you know I'm queer. My family owns a big farm outside of Montgomery, Alabama, and we grew up on that farm, all of us, working on that farm together. My dad and my uncles worked the farm together every Saturday. We went to church together on Sunday. So that's a big loss, that whole extended family, but maybe it's a part of growing older, too.

I tried. I have a beloved cousin, J. When we were kids, we'd make up these musical shows together and make our parents listen to them. When I was in my thirties, we were driving to a family reunion together. I tried to come out to him in the car. I started to bring it up, and he says, "No. Homosexuality is a sin, and I will not accept it. We just cannot talk about it," and that was the end of it.

When I was growing up, we went to church with my grandparents, Sunday morning, Sunday night, and Wednesday night. I loved church as a child. If the church had acted better, I wouldn't have had to hide from my family of origin all that time. I wasted a lot of years living a long way away from my mom, hiding. If the church had preached, "Your gay children are not sinning and are not going to hell, and you can accept your gay children," I could've come out to my family of origin a long time before I did. I could be closer to my family than I am now. I would not have moved away from the church. I wouldn't have lost that faith that I had as a kid. I'm not sure if I'll ever get it back.

I was in fourth grade when I was baptized. I remember my grandparents crying, so excited because I wasn't going to go to hell. But I had this innate sense that the church was wrong about this. I wasn't going to hell even before I was baptized, because if you say God made everything, then God made me. How can I go to hell? My faith was so strong.

If I had not been rejected by the church, maybe my faith

wouldn't have faded. Or maybe it would have. Maybe I would've grown and lived in other places and been exposed to other views and come to that realization without having to be gay. But being gay and ostracized by the church opened that door to my leaving. It's all intertwined: the church and not coming out to your family, the church and losing your faith.

As an adult I grew stronger in my beliefs about certain things. I was not going to support any organization that makes a woman a second-class citizen. I began to listen to what was coming out of preachers' mouths. That's when I stopped going. I didn't set foot in a church until Galileo, just a year ago.

Ava wanted to go to Galileo. I met with [Reverend] Katie [Hays] and told her I didn't really know if I believed in God anymore. Katie said, "Well, I'm an atheist about four times a week, so you'll be okay." I don't know what I believe anymore. I just muddle through, and Galileo makes it comfortable for me to muddle through my beliefs right now. I would love to get that faith back that I had as a child, but I don't know.

When I found out my nephew was gay—my sister and I were in her car and I said, "Have you noticed all of W.'s [her son's] friends are gay?" My sister said, "That would be because W. is gay." I burst into tears. My sister drove the car away as fast as she could because I'm crying in the driveway and W. was standing right there. She says, "What is wrong with you? Why are you crying?" I said, "Because his life will be so hard. His life will be so different. I don't want that for him."

As a young person, you have to be prepared that things could go really badly for you. But they might also be fine. If you hide in the closet, you're sending the message that there's shame associated with who you are and what you are. I have come to terms with my life and I am very happy. I have found the love of my life in Ava. I just took a long time to get here.

DOING THE WORK

Ava (she/her)

A va (she/her) is a physical therapist in her fifties, and she was recently married to Leanne (she/her), whose story immediately precedes this one.

Ava grew up in a family she describes as "solid," with a pastor father, a stay-at-home mother, and three older sisters. Acceptance of her being gay varied from person to person in her family of origin, with years of estrangement from her mother resulting, finally, in reconciliation.

Ava spent much of her young adulthood learning to accept herself so that others could accept her, too. She might have expected it would work in the opposite direction—other people's affirmation would lead to her own self-love. But she took on her share of what she calls "the work" and saw it bear fruit in her most important relationships.

MY FAMILY WAS SOLID. We had daily meals together. There were four girls in the family, sisters, and we were all so different from each other. I'm the youngest. I am the bouncy, extroverted, athletic, all-over-the-place kid, so totally different.

Mom and Dad taught us how to get along in society. Dad taught me how to work on my car. He taught one of my sisters how to work toward her theater interests. Both my parents really helped us develop our interests. We had an intact family with two parents, and we had support, and we had food, and we had a house.

But for some part of the coming-out process I was completely alone. I came out when I was seventeen. I knew earlier, but I didn't have words for it. But I knew. When I was seventeen, I confided in a camp counselor. The summer after I graduated high school, I came out to my mother. She had seen a long-distance telephone record and wanted to know what that two-hour phone call was all about. I said, "Well . . ." and, "Mom, I think I'm gay."

That was the start of some really difficult things with my mom and some beautiful things with my father. Mom had a cow; Dad did not. Mom was just beside herself. She was frantic. She was crying. She was very animated, tearful, and she kept on saying, "I have to call your father. I have to call your father." Dad was at the church. (My dad is a minister in the Disciples of Christ.) It was a weekday. So she called him.

I was nervous. I was like, "Oh God, here comes Dad. Here comes the minister, and the whole gay thing is wrong. I'm going to go to hell." He came in and assessed her crying and me crying and asked what was going on, and I choked out, "I think I'm gay." He came over to me and hugged me and said, "I love you and I always will."

The sister closest to me in age was very accepting, too. The other two were older than me by eight and ten years, and I didn't have as much relationship with them. The eldest didn't quite understand, but she was always there. The second-eldest, she had more of a difficult time. It took her a while. They've all been great supports and we've been on really good terms for many years.

Mom and I were estranged for probably seven, eight, nine years, something like that. I didn't have much contact with her. She couldn't do it because of whatever her background and her upbringing were. She just couldn't do it. Dad was the go-between. I didn't have much of a conversation or a relationship with her, but he was always right there.

When I came out, Mom said, "You're going to go talk to a

counselor." They chose a minister friend of theirs. I didn't come around to being straight the way he thought I would, and he said the words, "I'm disappointed in you." Honestly, I thought he was full of shit. I really didn't care what he felt. I didn't have the words for that then, but that was my attitude because I was just kind of figuring out this is who I am.

That pastor thought I needed further counseling, so referred me to a licensed professional counselor who was marvelous. She really helped me begin to talk through my relationship with my mother. She also advised me to read up on anything I could find about anything to do with being gay.

Talking about my mom with the counselor was difficult. Mom was, she just.... She really didn't.... She just couldn't get it. And it was not just not understanding intellectually, but emotionally in her spirit. It was almost the worst thing that could have happened for her. One time we were in the car—I don't know why we were talking about my being gay, but that was an ever-present discussion—and we were going somewhere, and I don't really remember the conversation, but she just acted out with the car. She was driving. She was almost screaming, being upset with me, and the car was going very fast all of a sudden. And I thought, *We're going to die.*

Another time she said the words, "You're dead to me." I was very wounded at the time. It took a long time to work that through, that she didn't really feel like she knew me anymore. I had been this daughter, I had been this person, and then all of a sudden here's this completely brand-new thing that she had no concept of. That's what she meant by, "You're dead to me." Not that she was going to write me out of the family. But it took me a long time to understand that. It was very wounding at the time.

Then I went to college. I was closeted when I was at Texas A&M. It was dicey, finding friends who would be open to me, and I lost some people that I thought were friends in the process. That taught me some things. There are people out there who you can or cannot trust, and you have to be wise about who you select to talk to. If they turn you down, maybe it's not about you. Maybe it is, but maybe it's also about what their insecurities are.

So I was a freshman at A&M. I went to the Sterling Evans Library and there was a section for all the gay literature. It had the letters HQ before everything and I laughed: homosexual, queer, HQ. I read everything I could find, history and old fiction and everything, and that was helpful to me, just learning what I could.

In about 2003, almost twenty years later, we were in Kansas. My father's mother was dying. My mother and I, we needed to get away from the house, so we went driving. It was snowing. It was evening. It was a late spring snow. Mom said she wanted to talk to me, and that always instilled a feeling of dread.

In the car, she said she wanted to apologize to me. I was stunned. She wanted to apologize to me for how difficult it had been between her and me. She said that she had been so scared. What had helped her along the way were some friends who had come to my parents and said their daughter was gay. Mom and Dad were able to say, "Well, what do you know? So is ours and here's our trip." They were able to be helpful to the other family, and that helped Mom somehow.

Four or five years after I graduated college, before my mom's apology, I stopped being nervous about being gay. I woke up one morning and I just wasn't worried about being gay. It just wasn't on my mind, "Am I saved?," all of that, it just was gone. Part of why it went away was my job at an AIDS project. I was around a lot of gay people and it was okay, and then it was like, "Well, maybe I'm okay, too." It just went away and then I commenced with life.

In my twenties and thirties I was this ardent, outspoken defender. "Don't say that. That's ridiculous. Gay people are just as . . ." But over time I had less need to confront people. I've been able to be still. It took a lot of therapy. And a lot of hot tea with milk in New England.

I did a lot of reading (and still do) about different religions, different ways of thought. I read up on Taoism. It has to do with being peaceful where you are, and this sense that you have to accept yourself. My life is less stressful because of it. I'm happier because I don't try to hook into the chaos.

So now I'm in a good place with myself, and with my family, which I know because we can be in the same room and laugh. I get to spend time with my nieces and nephews and their children. Leanne and I got married five weeks ago, and my nephew and his wife wanted their daughters to be at our wedding. They came and they were just like, "Wow. It's such a big, different world than we knew!"

I have a patient right now who has a family member. I'm not sure how close they are, but their relative is going through transition. My patient is female, and I'm not sure which direction the trans person is going, I didn't quite grab that. But the patient is just so perplexed. Her relative is a late teenager now, and my patient is in her mid-sixties or so. It's just completely foreign. She says, "This person grew up this way and we did all these things. . . . And now this person has a completely different life and doesn't talk to me anymore." And she says they go out all over town and stay in their room and are on the computer a lot. She doesn't know what to do with that.

I think people who are coming out have to make a conscious decision about how much relationship they want to have with each person in their family. Do you still want to have a relationship? Then you've got to bend, and that person's going to bend, too. But you've got to decide if you want to have a relationship or not. If you don't, then that's a different thing entirely.

I find, the more I am accepting of who I am, the more everybody else around me kind of just chills out. That's really been true of my family: when I stopped being anxious or worried, and I was just more relaxed with who I was, they were, too. They could see that I wasn't worked up, and they felt better about the situation.

So maybe that whole "I don't want to just be tolerated"—I think if people can work really hard, and find the helpers, and do a lot of work, and get to know themselves as individuals, things kind of settle down around them. A patient asked about my wedding ring. I told them, "My wife and I got married a month ago," and they didn't know what to do with that. But they're still coming to see me, so I think we're okay.

The work for me was being able to say, "I am attracted to women and that's just a fact of the matter. I really don't have any attraction to men." I just kept saying that until I was okay with it. And I had to say, "My mother is having a hard time with this," and say that out loud. And then, more work: "Who am I? Am I dependent upon other people, this or that relationship, for who I am or how I am?" So a lot of my life was learning to rely on myself and knowing what I could do; and if I couldn't do it, learning how to do something different. There's been a lot of reliance on myself, learning how to be reliant on myself. And relationships came from that.

If I could go back in time, I'd tell my seventeen-year-old self, "It's going to be okay. You're going to be okay. You'll do the work, and you're going to be okay."

PREPARE YOURSELF

Kyra (she/her)

Kyra (she/her) is in her twenties. She married Neve in 2014, who subsequently came out as transgender (MTF, or male-to-female), necessitating a shift in Kyra's self-understanding. Neve (she/her) was present in their home during Kyra's interview, not seated with the interviewer but sometimes passing through, making occasional comments; and at the end of the following narrative her contribution is noted.

Kyra recalls her and Neve's intentionality about achieving financial independence before their combined coming out. They knew their new identities would strain relationships with their extended family, perhaps severely enough to result in a loss of tangible support. They wanted to be confident and ready to stand strong together in their new, queer, married life.

Kyra is the daughter of Kellie and Daniel, whose story of Kyra and Neve's coming out immediately follows this one.

WHEN NEVE FIRST CAME OUT TO ME, we were by ourselves. I feel embarrassed for this now, but Neve had been trying to come out to me for years, and I was just ignorant. She was like, "What would you have done if I was a girl when you met me?" I'm like, "My family's super against that, so I probably wouldn't have talked to you." I just didn't realize that there was meaning behind her questions.

Eventually, she finally said, "No, I mean it. I'm a girl." By this point, I was lucky. When Neve finally really came out to me, I was deep in social justice circles. I was very close to my friend who had transitioned a couple of years before. I knew she had to transition. I knew there was no choice, and I had to be there for her because who else was going to be there? Her family sucks.

Neve has dyslexia, and her family never really helped with it. I was able to do research for her, about feeling like a girl, and that helped her realize, "Oh, other people experience this. Oh, that's trans. Interesting, okay." We helped each other in that regard.

Later on, we told a group of friends. We got kind of lucky; we made a new group of friends, none of whom had known Neve before she came out. She got to begin her transition with these friends, with them not knowing anything about her before.

For a while it was very segmented. Like, this person knows, but we're having to be fake with this person. We were living with my parents at the time. I didn't think that my parents were going to be unaccepting, but I knew it was going to be an emotional journey because of how religious my extended family is.

My parents go on vacation with my extended family every single year. My extended family is my grandparents, my cousins, my aunts, my uncles, everybody on my mom's side of the family. The year before we came out to them, I basically knew this was going to be the last time I would go on vacation with them. Gay marriage had just been legalized [June 2015]. It was in July, and my family decided to hold a prayer about that, everyone holding hands, because we were all so scared, because now gay people could get married. I literally was sweating, because I was thinking how much everyone there wanted to fight what was about to happen.

I wanted to wait until we moved out for my parents to find out. Our new goal became getting a job. Me and Neve both got jobs. We escaped the house, and literally that week, I told my parents. We built our own circle of support so that if we lost our family support, we'd be safe. I knew I had a home that I could afford, with a job, just in case. I never thought my parents were going to be assholes, but I thought the extended family might be horrible to them. I thought that people might be horrible to my mom, and the further I could get away from them, the safer they'd be from their family.

We told my parents, and we also told Neve's family of origin. Her family was always very abusive. So we chose her transition as a chance to cut off contact. We basically said, "Guess what, Mom and Dad? I'm a girl. Also, y'all are assholes. I don't care if you accept this or not because it's probably better if you don't."

My parents and my brother, they knew everything was going to be bad. I think Mom came out to Mamaw [Kyra's mother's mother] privately, and then the rest of the family found out through that. Everyone was upset. Everyone blamed my parents for not making us Christian enough to not be gay. That was hard.

My parents took care of the dirty work of coming out to the side of the family I knew was going to be a problem. They did that for me. That was emotional, and painful, and my parents have done so much. They've given us support, money, emotional help, guidance, everything. It didn't take them very long to come around. When they came around, it didn't take them long to find Galileo Church. My parents have been rock stars in regard to support. They've been Neve's parents, too. That's been our circle, basically.

I have two cousins who have chosen to contact me. I have another cousin who chose to speak to the Fort Worth school district to not allow trans people to go to the bathroom. I don't think I'm ever going to forgive him for that. I saw it online. I shouldn't have watched it, but I did. Hearing my oldest cousin saying all this after knowing that his cousin is married to a trans woman, literally calling trans people gross—it was really messed up.

But I've never gotten along with that side of the family. There was bullying. I remember being very young, and I asked what was wrong with my family. My mom actually said, "They're all chauvinists." Now I know what that means. It's a very traditional Texas view of masculine and feminine. All of the girls are in cheerleading, and super skinny, and super Christian, super straight. You have to fit exactly in these boxes, very small boxes. I've always been weird. I've always been an artist. I've always been different, and they've never liked that I didn't fit in.

They think that they're not being mean. They think they're being helpful. They're just asking questions. They're just worried about our souls. They have no idea how hurtful the jokes they make are. I found my uncle's Twitter and he posted a joke, misgendering a trans woman. He has no idea what a bully he is. Maybe he does. I don't know.

It wouldn't hurt my feelings if they never came around, but it would be a nice change if they did. It would be nice. I want to have relationships with some of my cousins. I want to have relationships with the children. Neve was always so close to the kids, my cousins' kids. They loved us, because we were silly, and we would play with them, and watch cartoons, and entertain them while the rest of the family was busy trying to look cool. We love those kids. They've always said we're welcome to come to any events where there are no children. At what family events are there no children? Every family event, there's children. And there's nothing wrong with us that we can't be around children.

My grandma, she has private dinners with us. She does well to not misgender or misname Neve, which is great, but she won't stand up to the rest of the family. Honestly, it's old-school sexism. When me and Neve first got married, she told me I needed to rely on Neve because women's prayers don't reach Jesus. They're anti-women being leaders of the church. So Neve transitioning to be a woman was even more messed up for them, because the more they accept Neve as a trans woman, the more they have to come to terms with me being gay. If they don't accept Neve, then I am still a straight girl. I'm still savable.

When I was a kid, I thought I had the best family in the world. We saw each other all the time. I know I had the best grandpa in the world, named B. [Kyra's nickname for him], who loved us. He treated me very well. He was very open-minded, and I can't help but wonder if he was alive now, if the family wouldn't have just cut us off like that. He would have made it different. He would have talked it out until he understood. He had my back.

That might be naive. He might have been confused and unable to grasp it. But I really feel like he listened to me more than any of them ever have. He was on my side when they weren't. There was a phrase that I could say if any of the cousins were being mean to me; I could yell it and he'd come get me. Didn't matter how old I was, he'd come get me.

A couple of years ago, my parents didn't want to go to a wedding that I wasn't allowed to go to. I had actually been invited to this wedding, but I told them I'm not going to any more family events without Neve. I tried that once, and they just acted like I was single. So it came as a really big surprise when my cousin texted me recently and invited me to her wedding. I told them we weren't going to come to any more events if it was just me, that I only want to come to events that Neve can come to.

My cousin said we're both invited, so we're going to go. My whole family will be there, and we'll see what happens. I am not having any expectations. I don't expect them to get better. It would be nice. But I'm actually very happy with the friends that I have. I have a very good chosen family. Having these friends who are there for me really helps with the family crap.

People on my dad's side of the family were all very supportive. My grandma on my dad's side of the family has Alzheimer's. She makes Christmas stockings for everyone in the family, and she had made Neve's years ago. She unstitched and restitched it with Neve's new name and said, "If I ever forget, I just want you to know that I was on your side." I cried. That was really powerful. I think that was the most powerful support in the beginning of our transition, from Grandma.

I feel confident in things that I know, when I know something for sure. That's something my grandpa used to say: "Remember what you know for sure." I was supposed to reply, "B. loves Kyra." That's something I still think about. Because no matter what, I know that for sure, that B. loved me. No matter what, I know for sure.

I also know these things for sure about Neve, about her gender. No one can make me doubt the choices I've made, because I have made them with education. The world is full of misinformation. For years, we got misinformed about trans stuff. We read all these toxic, horrible theories about trans people. But science supports trans people.

Practically speaking: you don't know when you're coming out. So start getting ready to be independent. You don't know when you're coming out who's going to be there for you. And no matter how bad it is, it's better to come out than to hold it in. Even when things were bad, even when my family was exploding, even when Mom was so emotional, saying, "Why? Why is this happening?," even during all of that, the relief of having come out and not keeping this a secret anymore was so much better. It's better. Come out. Be ready. Be safe. But come out.

Another thing about coming out: once you start, you don't stop. I hear some parents say, "I don't want my kid to ever come out." And that's unrealistic. The kid is going to have to come out. Maybe not to you, maybe they'll just tell you they have a girlfriend, and that's going to be the end of it. But they're going to have come out—to their grandparents, and they're going to have to come out to their job, and they're going to have to come out to people on the street, and people at a bar or a restaurant. Every single time I talk to someone, they're talking about their husband. Do I mention I have a wife? Do I mention she's trans? Do I mention . . . ? There's so many levels to myself that I have to keep under wraps or say publicly.

On social media, I am very, very public. I am very loud. I use a lot of social media, too, Twitter, Instagram, Facebook, all of it. I'm definitely not stealth in any of that. I'm constantly posting political things. I never saw myself as a political person before. But this is my life. This is stuff that's affecting me directly. Trans people need visibility. We need people to see.

My main source of support comes from friends, from online communities. I've been in the online world since I was very young. Part of being bullied all the time is that I made friends online. I found a support group called My Partner Is Trans, and it was a space where I could go and ask all the questions I needed to ask, questions I couldn't ask my wife, because she's the one going through the transition. Anytime I had concerns, or was excited about something, I was able to find support like that.

But I definitely censor myself in real life, because we are in Texas. Things are scary. There are times that it is scary to hold hands in public. I'm likely to censor myself if I'm alone, because there are people who are physically strong and scary. And it's a little scary seeing people stare at us and wonder. That's some scary stuff. It's fucking hard.

My first year of college I thought, "Oh, there's churches every two blocks. I feel very safe. I could go into any of these buildings, and I could find someone who could help me if I was ever in trouble." But I don't feel that anymore. When I see churches every two blocks, I feel scared. I feel unsafe. I feel like the people around me, if I got in trouble, if they realized anything about us, we would be in more danger.

It's very dangerous. You have to be safe to come out.

Here Neve adds, "What I did for myself before I started coming out is just sort of realize that I was going to make it, that I was going to get to transition. That thought gave me so much peace of mind. I was going to be good with whatever happened, because transition was at the other end. That's all I really needed to know the whole time. And there's a wealth of people waiting for you, in this life you're scared to live."

PERMANENT DISTANCE, NO GOING BACK

Daniel (he/him) and Kellie (she/her)

Daniel (he/him) and Kellie (she/her) have two adult children, A. (he/him) and Kyra (she/her). Kyra married Neve (she/her), an MTF trans woman who transitioned a few years into their marriage. Kyra's story immediately precedes this one.

Neve's coming out activated deep protective instincts in Kellie and Daniel. Daniel's family of origin was mostly kind and supportive, but Kellie's family responded to Neve with stubborn hostility and fear born of religious conviction. Kellie and Daniel have found themselves pulled between a close-knit extended family that excludes and belittles Neve, and their children, of whom they now count Neve as one.

But they have witnessed a softening of hearts on both sides. Some members of Kellie's family are gradually more accepting of Neve; and Kyra and Neve are at peace with not always being included. Daniel and Kellie have changed, too; their initial confusion has been replaced by activism as a sign of love for all their children.

Daniel

I was outside working by myself. This is right before Thanksgiving 2014, and Kyra and Neve, but then we knew Neve by her old name, they both came out and said, "Hey, can we talk to you?" Uh-oh. That's never good. They had been living with us for a while at that point. Neve was estranged from her family. Kellie and I didn't know why they were having issues.

I said, "Sure, what's up?" They didn't hem and haw about it. Kyra was doing most of the talking. She said, "You know I was having trouble for a long time, and not really knowing what it was. Well now we figured out what it is." And then she said that Neve, who we knew as our daughter's husband, was transgender. I was like, "Whoa, whoa."

I knew what transgender was but I didn't know very much about it. My first question was, "What does this mean about your relationship? Are you still interested in my daughter, in being married to her?" They said yes, they were both still very interested, they still loved each other. Kyra said, "This was a shock for me at first but I've had time and we've known about this for a while." They told me that they had already been seeking counseling.

It wasn't a long conversation, really. They were ready to leave. They said, "And would you tell Mom? Thanks. Bye."

I was not looking forward to this. I sat there and I sat there and asked myself, "How long can I delay this?" But Kellie knew something was up because I was being real quiet. So I said something like, "I have some really weird news to tell you."

Kellie

The saddest thing to me, looking back, is that my reaction was out of worry for what my family was going to do, 100 percent. It was going to destroy my mom. My family wasn't going to deal well. I reacted out of all the fear of having to deal with them and hurting my mom. I always felt responsible for my mom.

It makes me sad hearing that Daniel's first thoughts were, "What does this mean for your relationship," thinking of Kyra, and my first thought was protecting my mom. That's the stress.

I was immediately dreading that because we were going to be in the middle. And we knew it.

It took me probably three days to get to where I was okay. I was upset and crying most of the time, just because of the fear of having to deal with this. My family is very much in each other's business, and vocal with their opinions, and bossy. I knew there was going to be an attack on us as parents.

We didn't tell my family for months. We decided to wait through the holidays, kind of giving them a last "normal" holiday. But right after Christmas, Kyra and Neve were ready to tell. Neve was having to dress "straight" for those events, but she had already started growing her hair out. I remember Mom giving her a hard time about her hair, saying she needed to cut it. "After the holidays," we told them really fast.

I called them all together. I had my brothers and my nephew, and I think my niece was invited but I had already told her. We sat them down. At the time we were very confused by it and I think we were really honest about that. I said, "They're happy, they're doing well, we love them, but we don't understand this. We don't know why because we really don't know a lot about it."

One of the things my brother said was, "Maybe it's just a fad that he's choosing to do for now." And I'm like, "No. It's not like cross-dressing, you know."

Daniel

My family is not in everybody's business. My family mostly was accepting. I told my mother before I told my father because I knew where she stands on things. She's fairly liberal but she's been in a really conservative church forever. I know that has some impact. So I told her, and she said okay, she had questions. She said, "They're not still married anymore, are they?" I said, "Yes, Mother."

She said, "But they're not intimate." I said, "Yes, Mother, not that that's any of our business."

Kellie

She's still convinced that they're just friends.

Daniel

I told my mother, "I think I want you to tell Dad." She said, "Okay, I know how to tell him." She told me later what she said: "G., you remember how when you first met [Neve's former name] and you thought he was really effeminate? You were *right!*" So he got to be right and to find out this news. He's a very loving and accepting person. He may not agree but he is not going to disown you. They were just like, "That's cool. Whatever."

Kellie

Daniel's sister and brother-in-law are doctors, so they were like, "This is a real thing. Like, medically, this is a thing." Because we were still learning about it. We asked them, "Have you come across this? What are your opinions?"

Daniel's dad said, "They're always welcome at our house." And so that next Christmas—this is so weird because when I go back, the pronouns get messed up and it's [Neve's former name] still in my head. It's frustrating to me because we don't ever go there. I hate having [Neve's former name] pop into my head.

Anyway, that next Christmas, Daniel's parents invited the kids to their house for Christmas just like normal. My family did not. Neve was only welcome with my family if Neve came as [Neve's former name]. They said they didn't want Neve around the little ones.

For two years, they all decided not to use the name Neve, or her pronouns, because they had heard some online pastor say that you're actually causing someone to sin if you support it. After a couple of years of this, we had a big blowup with my family. We tried to have a family meeting about it. We got everyone together at my office and started talking about Neve. We were asking, "How can we have her be a part of this family? She really wants to, because she misses you all."

Daniel

This started because everybody was frustrated. They were frustrated with us because we wouldn't show up to certain things. And we were like, "Well, we don't go to things when our whole family is not invited."

Kellie

Neve would not be invited. Kyra and A. would be, but not Neve. My nephew got married and we did not go to the wedding or the rehearsal dinner. I helped decorate but I didn't go. It was so fresh and hurtful to Kyra. We were torn. We did not know how to be good, loving parents, and still go to something where they were not invited. We were still learning how we were going to navigate this family.

After the wedding, we had this big meeting because there were some hurt feelings. It didn't go well. Immediately my sister-in-law said, "I just feel like it's a sin and I have to speak the truth to them, so if I see them I'm going to speak the truth to them." My nephew said, "What do you want us to do? I don't want my children around that. I don't want them to know." Blah blah blah. There was a lot of attacking happening, and I just lost my shit.

Everyone started yelling stuff, and I just yelled, "Shut the fuck up!" But you do not say "fuck" in my family. They all said, "Oh, I don't have to listen to this," and everyone got up and left. Later I did apologize because I knew that's an offensive word to them. I said, "I'm not sorry for how I felt. I'm sorry for what I said to you." There's a permanent distance there. I mean, we're just not really close to anybody anymore. There's a lot of family texting, joking, and we're not in on that anymore.

My niece is getting married next week. Neve was actually invited to her wedding shower. It's the first family function since 2015 that Neve's been invited to. It was all women and it was great and nobody knew. I think they had gotten so worked up that it would be so horrible. Somebody asked Neve who she was and she said, "I'm Kellie's daughter-in-law." And it was fine!

We've been talking to the kids and we decided, because of the relationship that I had with my mom and dad and the problems my mother has in her life, that we're going to try to do the stuff we can do for her. If that means going to some things without Neve for a little while, then we will. Because Kyra and Neve at this point are fine. When they get invited to stuff they're thrilled. But they have let go of most of those relationships.

Over time, my mom has changed more and more. She and I have had several talks over the years and she's totally changed. It helped that my niece, the one who has the little kids that they're all worried about being around Neve, went to counseling. Her counselor, who is a conservative Christian counselor, told her it's damaging and disrespectful to not use the right name. The right name for that person is the name they've asked you to use.

After that my mom started trying to use Neve's name and trying the pronouns, realizing this was not going to go away. Neve was not going away. Mom did not want to lose Kyra and A. I still think to this day, my mom would be fine if Neve disappeared. Her main focus is Kyra and A. But she does have Neve over and she's very nice to her. She's been trying to hold that relationship together. They've all decided that they need to support Kyra and A. because they still feel like they're trying to save Kyra and A.

Daniel

Kellie's dad was a huge unifier of the family. When he died the family was kind of left without a leader. He was so incredibly strong. He would say, "This is what we're doing!" and everybody fell into line. We have wondered what this transition would've looked like had Kellie's dad still been alive. I don't know the answer.

Kellie

Yeah. He always ended up, as strong as he was, on loving people. My heart tells me that he would have said, "I worry about Kyra, I love Kyra, I love you all, now everybody get over it. Because Kyra is our child." But for us, Neve's like one of our children.

Daniel

We really kind of took on Neve as our child when her family was so terrible to her, before we even knew why they were so terrible. We knew that Neve had gone through lots of counseling as a kid and was troubled in some ways, got in trouble at school.

But one day, Kyra said, "I want you to listen to this voicemail that Neve's parents left." Kyra and Neve had stopped talking to Neve's parents because it was harmful and gross. Neve's dad left a message saying, "Where's [Neve's former name]? Why aren't y'all talking to us? Is he wearing girl's clothes again?" It turns out they always knew about Neve thinking that she was transgender. They knew, they *knew*.

Kellie

Her whole life, she dressed up in her sister's clothes. She was always in trouble for it, shamed for it. Neve's siblings are influenced by their parents and by friends who are not accepting. At first they said, "We love you, we support you." Then they backed off and didn't have anything to do with her.

Now Neve calls us Mom and Dad. I feel protective of her. I feel like this is someone who's very important to my child. She has been hurt, like a baby bird, and I'm going to protect this person and march in marches and do whatever I can to make sure that this person is not hurt any more, by anyone.

I don't think she knows what it's like to have a really loving, close relationship with a mother. Our relationship is really very different but I think she loves it. Just the fact that we go to Galileo and wear Pride shirts is enough to make her feel loved and accepted as a child.

I want to say to people, "Be kind, because your heart may change over time. Take it slow, because the things that come out of your mouth today may be very harmful for a long time. You may soften how you feel in a year or two when you really think about this and pray about this and study this."

And I want people to know how serious this is. We're dealing with suicide. If Neve had killed herself, which she might have, I would never have been able to talk to my family [of origin] ever again. I think people don't realize that this is someone's life, and they're already depressed, they've already been fighting this their whole life, and they're on the line.

Daniel

I wish, looking back, Neve could have come out sooner. When they were dating, Kyra could have said, "This is the person I love." I think that would have been an easier transition. But no, I would never go back, because our life is just so much better now.

SOMETIMES IT GETS BETTER, SOMETIMES IT GETS WORSE

Rory (they/them)

Rory (they/them) is in their twenties and recently married to Noah (she/her), whose story is shared elsewhere in this book. Rory is the daughter of Jackie (she/her) and the child-in-law of Karen (she/her) and Kurt (he/him), whose stories follow this one. Rory is in college and has plans to enter seminary to study for Christian ministry.

Rory's coming out happened in stages: first a declaration of bisexuality, broadening later to pansexuality; then a recognition of their gender fluidity. They see this as a point of connection with the people they've come out to, because people's reactions to Rory's queerness also evolve over time—sometimes for the better, sometimes for the worse.

Rory describes the loss of a wide extended family over a period of several years. Even relatives that might be allies can't remain in relationship with them: "I don't want [my cousins] to have to pick sides." And Rory is well aware that their gender identity, or rather their mother's acceptance of it and their father's refusal to accept it, factored in the dissolution of their parents' marriage.

But Rory's own fluidity of identity allows for the possibility that even broken relationships can be reconciled: "Not everything has to be an ultimatum."

I DIDN'T REALIZE I was on the rainbow until I moved out of my parents' house. I was eighteen or nineteen. When I first realized that I was somehow not perfectly straight, it was the third or fourth time in pretty close succession that I had looked at a woman and thought, "Oh, if I was gay, I would think she's really pretty." And then I just, at some point, was like, "Yeah, I've been saying that a lot lately." And I guess it was the Holy Spirit; me not being straight was the first step to finding my own self that was always in there.

I'm thinking about the several times that I came out. It was not just once and done. It was over and over again. Not only that, but each person I came out to had multiple reactions. There was their immediate reaction and then there was their later reaction and sometimes a third, and sometimes one was nicer or meaner than the other. The best thing is when it gradually gets nicer. But some people, immediately they're like, "Oh, of course, I still love you," and then later, they're way meaner about it.

The more people that I told before I got to my family of origin, the more real it felt. You read about people who come out and about queer people's experiences, and it feels strange the first time you claim that as your own. But once I had told it a couple of times, it started to feel like my own story.

I told my mom first, accidentally. We had gone to a big family reunion and none of them knew. At the reunion I felt more and more exhausted as the day went on, because I felt like I was pretending. It was wearing on me.

I rode with my parents. I was ready to get out of there and go home so I could be by myself and be my own self. Then I realized I had left my purse with my keys in it at the family reunion. We had to drive back up there. So here I am in the car with my mom and I'm like, "Oh my gosh, I thought this was over," and I started weeping. I just blurted it out: "I'm bi"—my label has changed several times—"and I don't think it's a sin, and I just had to tell you." She was very kind. She didn't agree with me theologically at the time.

She said, "If you're bi, couldn't you just only date guys?" I could tell it was hard for her to understand.

She said that she and Dad had discussed this: "What would we do if one of our kids was queer?" Of course, they wouldn't have said "queer." What they agreed on is that they wanted to be a part of our lives no matter who we were. And they wanted people important to us to be a part of their lives. It felt like a consolation prize, but still much, much better than a lot of possible reactions. What I was more worried about was that once I told my mom, I'd have to tell my dad, because I could not ask her to keep that secret for a long time. And I knew, because I know my dad, that even though he was in that conversation with her, my dad acts very different in the practical than he does in the abstract. My mom does not.

I told one sibling at a time. I told two of my siblings before I told my dad and told the youngest after I told my dad because I didn't want to ask him to keep a secret from Dad. The older two siblings both said, "I don't really know what I believe. I've been hearing things and it's not as clear as when we were growing up. I know I love you, and I'll love you whatever you do." My youngest sibling said, "I don't agree," but, much like my mom, said, "I love you anyway and will love you no matter what."

I asked my mom to tell my dad right after that. I know that my dad's first reaction to things is often very emotional. He often says things he doesn't mean or later wishes he hadn't said. He just doesn't do well with surprises. So I asked her to tell him, and she did. It was the day after Christmas. I didn't want to ruin Christmas.

He called me the next day. He wanted to come over to my apartment. I knew that she had told him and that's what this was about. First thing, he hugged me and he said, "I love you no matter what." Very dramatic, very emotional. "I love you, no matter what! But. . . ."

And then it wasn't even logical the way he went on. He was pacing. He was rambling and ranting. I wasn't frightened, but his mind was clearly not in a rational place. It was very intense. He said, "Who decides what's right and what's wrong?" And I said, "Jesus." And he looked at me like I was crazy, like he did not even understand what I had said. I said, "I know you think that those couple of verses forbid all of it completely, but there are explanations around each one. And I could go through them but I'm not going to right now because I don't think that's what you want to hear."

He also told me, during this weird, long rant, some things I had never known about him, including that he was molested by older boys from when he was three years old. The way he described it was, "I was an active participant in the homosexual lifestyle between the ages of three and fourteen." I said, "Dad, there is no homosexual lifestyle between the ages of three and fourteen." What liberated him from that was the church's doctrine of antihomosexuality, in his view. All the pain he suffered his whole childhood, he explained it as, "Gay sex is broken," and that's why it hurt him. I could see that he didn't want me to go through that.

That conversation ended—*conversation* is a generous word—when I said, "Dad, I want to talk to you about all of this but not right now. You need to go." He was crying. We did talk about it later. It was never as freaking-out as it had been originally, but he also never really honestly considered things that I was saying. I really did my homework on the theology part.

My mom did, too, over the next couple of years. She read and read and read. She gave things to Dad that he read but that never struck him the same way. At one point my mom was convinced that at least it was not as clear as she had been told. Dad could not even conceive that. It was crystal clear to him.

I think it's partly because of his abuse trauma. If he starts to believe that it's not wrong, he has to cope again with his trauma. He would have to unpack that and change the way he tells that story in his own mind, change the way he copes with his past, which is a lot to ask of anyone.

My parents are divorced now. There were so many factors involved in that, including my coming out, but also so much more than that. The way my mom has described it is that my coming out shed some light on the shit that was already in her marriage.

I don't quite remember how I came out to my grandparents. I think I might have written them an email, in letter format but sent electronically. That's what I did with several people from my old church, people who were important to me. At some point I said, "Okay, the people who I need to tell specifically all know, and now it's going to go on social media. Let the grapevine do its work." But before I unleashed that, I sent a lot of letters via email. I wanted to give them a chance to respond to me, especially the ones who I believed would respond kindly. If they just saw it on Facebook, I don't know if they would have reached out to me with that kindness.

My mom, over the next couple years, would go back sometimes and apologize for initial reactions that I knew were only out of ignorance, not out of meanness. Once she had educated herself, she realized, "Oh gosh, something I said is not a thing you're supposed to say." She would apologize. For some people it was like that. They got kinder because they got more educated.

My uncle, my mom's brother, was one of the really terrible switches. He found out from the family that I was gay or queer or whatever I was saying then. He didn't say anything to me. He never brought it up. We had a couple of family gatherings after I had come out where things were fine.

Then my mom and my younger siblings went to my uncle's house in Galveston to play at the beach. My mom and her brother were out on the patio late one night, drinking and having a really good conversation. They talked about their childhood. For hours and hours they talked, late into the night. Then something came up about

Mom going to a new church now and that she's changed her beliefs a lot. And he said, "Yeah, I was wondering if you came over here to talk to me about that." She said, "Well, I can tell you my story if you want. I'm not here to convince you of anything. But if you're curious, I can tell you my story." He said, "Yeah, yeah. I want to know."

But when she started talking, he turned. "You can't come over here to preach at me and try to change my mind." He doesn't go to church. His objections aren't as religious as he wants to say they are. But, "If that was my kid, my kid would always be welcome in my house, but I would not let their partner in my house. I definitely wouldn't let any kids in my house. They wouldn't be my grandkids, because they can't have kids." Then he says that's his rule with me, too. I'm allowed to come over, but Noah isn't, and any kids we might have won't be. It had been two years or more since I had come out. None of this deep bigotry had come up before.

I've never had conversations about theology with my cousins. The one that's my age is probably the most religious of any of them. She goes to a conservative church, but I've never gotten the impression that she really lines up with everything they say. She's always been kind, and she actually apologized to me at her wedding: "I'm sorry Noah wasn't invited, it wasn't for any . . . reason. It's just when we sent out the invites y'all hadn't been dating very long."

Some distant family members really talked bad about my family and me on social media, to the point that we didn't go anymore to the big family reunion. My oldest cousin told me that was really disappointing for her. She said, "People who you grow up thinking love you, and then you realize that they only love you because you're a certain way—that means they don't really love me either because they wouldn't love me if I was gay."

I don't see my cousins much anymore because of my uncle. That has complicated things with his kids, who were always kind, because of course they still love their dad. I don't want them to have to pick sides.

I had a long email exchange with my grandparents about pronouns. They met Noah once before the explosion with my uncle. They came over to my mom's and we played Trivial Pursuit and had a good time. Noah fit right in. She's funny and my granddad is funny. He likes funny people. I think they enjoyed her company.

The next day my granddad started talking about Noah and was saying she/her, using her pronouns. "She just fit right in. I really enjoyed talking to her." It all seemed great. But my mom told her parents about that big fight with her brother, which of course made my grandmother cry. She just hates that her family doesn't all get along. She won't say who's at fault.. She won't take sides even in such a clear case. They talked to my uncle and the next time they talked to my mom they weren't using Noah's pronouns. They kept insisting that they were forgetting, but also insisting that they were going to forget. My granddad said, "Well, now don't get me on the pronouns, but he . . . ," and my mom said, "Okay, Dad, are you forgetting or is this intentional? Because that sounded intentional." He said, "Well, Jackie, he's a man." She said, "Okay, I think we're done here."

She told Noah and me about that conversation. I wish she hadn't told us. I think they were working through some things. They had talked to my uncle, and they took some things he said to heart, but then they took some more time, and since then they've improved. I think if we didn't know about that conversation, their improvement would be enough, especially for Noah. She has higher standards than I do for how other people behave toward us.

But Noah doesn't have the warm feelings towards them that I do, the memories of years of kindness and generosity and family. All she knows of them is that one Trivial Pursuit night and then the trouble about pronouns. Noah's granddad called her, wanting us to come over and spend the night and hang out. When she got off the phone I said, "Noah, do your grandparents always use your pronouns?" She said, "I don't know, but they love me." I said, "Well, that's how I feel about my grandparents."

I hear about my grandparents saying Noah's a man, and that is deeply hurtful to us both. But I don't have to decide, "These are the conditions. We're not going to spend time with you again unless these requirements are met." I could just take my time, not spend time with them for a while, and not make a big statement about it. Not everything has to be an ultimatum.

SMELLING THE SHIT
THAT WAS ALWAYS THERE

Jackie (she/her)

Jackie (she/her) is the mother of Rory (they/them), who is gender-fluid. Rory is recently married to Noah (she/her), who is gender-queer. Rory and Noah's stories are told elsewhere in this book.

In the years since Rory came out, Jackie and her husband have divorced, Jackie has left her evangelical church, and her extended family has gotten much smaller as she gauges each relationship for its integrity and value. She describes her role in the extended family as a "buffer," protective of her child and willing to sever relationships to ensure Rory and Noah's safety.

Even before Rory came out, Jackie had shown a willingness, in discussions with her kids about civil rights and churches, to be challenged by them, to take their questions seriously, to open her mind, and consider she had a blind spot. Jackie is honest about the distance she has traveled to be her child's strongest advocate, wishing she had done some of the theological, emotional, and practical work of LGBTQ+ inclusion before it was necessitated by learning of Rory's identity. She says she's glad, now, for the disruption this has caused, as she's able to see, finally, where the fissures in her marriage and family life were already present and deepening.

CHAOTIC DARKNESS. That's what it felt like about four years ago when Rory first spoke the words: "I think I might be bi." I was coming from a very conservative, evangelical background. Nothing had really prepared me for this.

I didn't know what to do with the information. I did not see it coming, and yet when they said it I wasn't surprised. For a minute I left my body and was kind of floating. I was brought back to myself when I noticed what Rory was saying: "Can I still come over to our house? Can I still see my siblings? Will you still talk to me? If I have a partner who is a woman, will you meet her? If we have children, will you have anything to do with them?"

I was immediately brought out of my own feelings. I had to set those aside because Rory thought they were losing their entire family. They thought they were losing me. I immediately switched gears into, "I don't know how I'm going to figure all this out, but right now they need to know that I love them, and they're not losing me."

There was this period of self-protection, and then I slowly started educating myself, deconstructing my beliefs. At first I had to say, "Okay, I'm not changing my beliefs right now." I had to work out, "What does it look like to love Rory right where I am?" I focused on that: that Rory is still our daughter, we still love Rory, and what does that look like?

Initially there was this struggle between us, because Rory wanted to be who they were fully, but they wanted to bring me with them. I couldn't get there right away, and I remember feeling very pressured by Rory. They kept wanting to have these conversations. I kept resisting, like, "You can't push me into this."

A friend from Galileo Church told Rory, "I think if you back off and don't pressure your mom, and give her time, she will eventually be one of your biggest allies. But you've got to back off." That turned out to be true.

I read several books, some of them affirming, some of them

not. The focus of one was on simply having peaceful conversations and loving each other, even when the parent is nonaffirming. But even in the nonaffirming books, the biblical argument that remained against being gay was so thin. When I looked at the harm that is done, the pain that is endured, the unhealth in queer people's lives, all based on this one tiny thread of scripture, there's no way I could justify that.

I still knew that Rory wanted me to be affirming. I remember the thought, "I want to be affirming, I want to believe that this is not a sin, I'm just not there yet, and you can't force yourself to believe something, even if you want to." It just took time. I woke up one day and was like, "Yeah. I'm not there anymore." It was time, and reading more things, and listening to more people, and processing it more.

Rory says their first coming out was as a feminist, which is funny but also true. It rocked a lot of our family boats for Rory to identify as a feminist. Then coming out as bi—they say now they really identified as pan, but they didn't know if I understood those words, and they didn't want to have that conversation. Later they said they identified more as a lesbian. Then they fell in love with Noah, who is not gender-binary. Noah's gender-queer. Then they said, "Well I can't really call myself a lesbian. I'm just going to say queer." Then they, Rory, came out as gender-fluid. How many is that?

The first time I asked, "Well, if you're bi, if you could go either way, why don't you just date a guy?" Which to me felt like a pragmatic question, because your life would just be way easier—though now I understand it was painful for Rory, and I regret asking it. Coming out as a lesbian, and then as queer, those didn't really matter to me at that point. The gender-fluid one was a little harder, because I had less understanding of it. I felt protective. I didn't want them to get hurt. I know that persecution is much worse for trans people.

I read some tips for parents about how to handle the coming-out conversation. I read that and thought, "I wish I had known these when Rory came out as bi." Then Rory came out as other things, finally gender-fluid. I said, "I'm so glad I had another opportunity to handle this right." This time I was able to focus on Rory, on reassuring them of my love and support, saving my questions for later. It's fair to have questions and concerns, but save that for a separate conversation. Let the first one be, "I support you, I love you," completely focused on them feeling supported.

Negotiating family-of-origin relationships was my job. I had to keep Rory at the center, because ultimately it is their story, it is their identity, and nothing I'm going through is as hard as what they're going through. At the same time, it's kind of a helpless feeling, that I am paying an immense cost for something that I did not choose. Part of that was being the buffer to my husband; part of that was being the explainer, the educator, with the extended family.

My husband and I had had these conversations before. What would happen if we had a gay kid? Where we landed was, we would still love them. But my interpretation of what that meant was very different from his. My husband was not affirming, not supportive. That first time especially, Rory didn't want me to tell him. I was going to have to hide this from my husband, and it was emotional for me to keep it from him. At the same time I dreaded him finding out, because I knew there was going to be this emotional outburst, and it was my job to be the buffer between him and the kids. That was going to require a lot of work, a lot of pain on my part, to handle him.

I had fear of rejection, fear of losing approval, and honestly, fear of losing the love, the affection, the support of all of these people. A fear of losing my identity, honestly. Because my identity was wrapped up in my beliefs about God. To change those beliefs, it had a domino effect on my entire life. I had fear of changing who I was, and feeling like, "Who am I anymore?"

Rory moved to another town, another church. Rory stepped out of our whole world. There was a time—I'm not proud of this—but I kind of resented that. It felt like Rory got to step out and leave me to clean up the mess. Obviously, that's not fair. But I remember feeling that way. Literally everywhere I went I was running into people we knew and having to think, "Okay, do they know? Do I mention it? What are they thinking?"

There were people that I realized really quickly I was going to have to pretty much cut off relationship with them. There were some people I was going to have to stay in a relationship with but put up firm boundaries. And there were some people I could just have loving conversations with, because they genuinely wanted to listen and hear and consider what I was saying.

There were such varying degrees of that, so I was having to figure out what to do with each person and then play these different roles. You think this is going to be a one-time event. You're going to come out and you're going to lose some people, and some people are going to stick. Then we'll be done. But it's not that way.

An aunt and uncle of mine had been cruel to Rory on Facebook. As a result I said to my grandmother, "We're not coming to Christmas, because it's just too hostile." My grandmother is one of the strongest people I know, and this was one of the very few times I saw her cry—not just cry, but sob. That was such a hard conversation.

I noticed that the times I reacted to Rory, or to situations surrounding Rory, in ways that I later regretted, I was acting out of fear. The way I handle these situations and conversations is almost always a choice between acting out of love or acting out of fear. It really is that simple.

I found out there are people who initially stick and fall away later, because it turns out they're totally cool with you being that way, but they don't want to hear about it. They don't want you "shoving it in their face." They fall away later. There are also people who fall away immediately and later come back.

My friend that I see once a month, she's nonaffirming, and it's not okay, but I feel like there is hope that she will listen and reconsider. It feels like it's okay to let that go for now. She could change later. With my parents, though, I was very firm on boundaries with pronouns, because my parents were giving pushback, and it was very important to draw this firm boundary and say, "This is how we are handling this, and it is not acceptable to do anything else." But that's family, that's not someone I see just once a month.

So I have to constantly evaluate, "What is this relationship, what's the cost, do I have the energy to have this conversation, and at what level?" An uncle—one of the ones that was so hostile on Facebook—I just cut out. His daughter is affirming, very supportive, and she's one of the few family members that I'm still close to. She said, "I wish y'all could make up, I wish y'all could reconcile." I said, "You know, that would be a sweet story. But the thing is, it requires so much energy." This is an uncle that, at our best, I saw once a year. We said, "Hello"; we hugged; we said, "How are you doing?" It feels cold to put people in categories like that, but I had to.

Noah [Rory's spouse] is gender-queer, male name, female pronouns. My mom asked, "Okay, but what is Noah really?" I said, "Well, Noah is gender-queer; again, this means she doesn't identify as fully male or female." She says, "Okay, but what was Noah born?" I said, "So, I used to ask questions like these too, and I understand your curiosity. But what I didn't know and now I do know is that it is considered rude to ask such questions, because essentially you're asking what's in Noah's pants." She said, "But, I mean, is Noah her original name?" I said, "This feels like another way of asking the same question. Again, to try to put it into perspective, you would never ask a man, 'Hey, how you functioning down there,' right?"

She said, "So if they were to get married, would they be able to have biological children?" I said, "So again, I'm not going to answer that." I mean, that's how blunt I had to get about drawing this very hard boundary around inappropriate questions I will not answer.

By contrast, someone at my internship asked about my kids. I said, "I have four. My oldest is gender-fluid, and I have two sons and a daughter." She was like, "Oh wait, what? What does that mean?" I started explaining it, and I could sense that this was genuinely so far out of her experience that knowing details would help her put this together. It felt like her intentions were good. It's interesting that I would tell this stranger stuff I wouldn't tell my mom. But drawing boundaries! So important.

Before, I didn't see my extended family, my life, as clearly as I do now. All of a sudden I started seeing all these things that I hadn't seen before. Rory being gay didn't cause any shit in my life, but it caused me to smell a lot of the shit that had always been there. My marriage had been bad for a long time. My ex-husband says Rory coming out and my older son's addiction—these things harmed our marriage. I don't think they did. I think they brought to light issues that were already there. You can hobble along with a broken leg sometimes, until you really need to use it. Then it becomes obvious that it's broken.

At first I needed to have answers on the theology surrounding being gay. And immediately upon finding the answers, I realized I don't care. Now what I keep saying to other parents is, "Don't wait until your kid comes out to think about these things." Because by the time I realized so many things, I had already done the damage. I wish people would think about these things before they have to.

Our church is so affirming and really centers queer people as we should. But as a result, you have parents and families who go to worship and they're not centered, because we're centering the queer people. That's hard sometimes. I've seen moms like myself who, when their kids come out, they're supportive, they're affirming, they become their kids' biggest fan, and they're cheerleading, and they're supporting, and they're helping their kids through surgeries and through major life events. They're fielding questions from the family, and losing their support systems, and having their own kind of crises happening. And having to defend their kid, realizing, "I have to get politically involved; my kid's life depends on this." All these things take so much energy. You bear such a beating, and then the mom burns out and emotionally tanks.

I remember saying all my life that my family was so close. We kept in touch with distant relatives. We would all get together and have these perfect Christmases, and everyone loved each other and forgave each other and got along. They would say, "Oh, family's family. You always love family no matter what." I just assumed that that's how we would treat my gay kid, and what I started seeing is that there were limits to these things that they believed about themselves. Having a gay kid was the limit. And then, after my brother said terrible things about Rory and Noah, refused to have Noah in his home, and called her terrible slurs, I was the one expected to apologize, and I saw that this is always the way my family has done things, that someone acts abusive and the family tolerates the abuse, and they ask the abused to smooth it over and make peace.

So some of the losses are people who outright reject your kid, and some of the losses are seeing someone in a completely different light, someone that you loved and cherished and was an important part of your life. Seeing those flaws in them and having them reject your kid is just very, very painful.

This is one of the best things that's ever happened to me. Honestly. That feels like a selfish statement, because this is Rory's thing, not mine. But it brought about so many good things in my life. That marriage needed to die; it was toxic. Now my kids and their partners and I have family get-togethers, and we laugh, and we talk, and we enjoy each other. It really is like I thought my family was before, but it wasn't. Finally seeing it—that never would have happened if Rory hadn't come out. I probably would have stayed in that marriage. I keep thinking, "I could have missed all of this" had Rory not come out, and had I not chosen what I did.

THE MAMA BEAR AND THE INTERPRETER

Karen (she/her) and Kurt (he/him)

Karen (she/her) and Kurt (he/him) have two adult children. Their elder child, Noah (she/her), came out as gender-queer shortly before graduating from college; and recently married Rory (they/them), who identifies as gender-fluid. Noah's and Rory's stories are presented elsewhere in this book.

Both Karen and Kurt grew up in a very conserving Christian denomination. Karen's father was a minister, and she separated from the church of her youth long before Noah's coming out. She teaches in a conserving Christian private school. Kurt maintains an active relationship with a conserving congregation where he has friends and influence, and he engages with Galileo Church faithfully as well. He is a specialist in biblical languages and works as a consultant for Bible translation projects.

They find themselves navigating the zone between Noah and those who will not accept her identity—at work, at church, and especially in their extended families. It is not a role they anticipated, but one they have taken up for the sake of the child they both love.

Kurt

For me, it was after church on a Sunday night, dropping her off in front of the university student center. We pulled up in the little circle drive there, and before she got out of the car, she said, "Oh, by the way, Dad, there's something that I need to tell you."

I was not really aware of the term *gender-queer* at the time. She gave some explanation about that, and I said something like, "Well, I can appreciate that feeling of not conforming to societal expectations about masculinity or what a 'real man' is." I didn't play team sports in school. I went deer-hunting a few times with my dad when I was in high school, but I never was a big outdoorsman. And I'm not a businessman, like most of my friends at church. I said something along that line. And affirmed my love and support for Noah.

A few weeks later, I asked: "I hope my response was okay." Noah said, "Yeah, that was fine. It was great." So at least the initial interaction was okay from Noah's end. It didn't come across as a negative, or disapproval, or whatever.

That was the fall of 2015. In 2016, she played cello at the Gay Christian Network conference, and she was obviously gender-nonconforming. She still had her beard at that point but was wearing a skirt on stage there. In the fall of 2016, she was wanting to come out to our extended family. We put that off, and we didn't end up going to family holiday dinners at all that year due to sickness in our family.

For a long time, I didn't know where Noah was going with all of this. She talked about liking feminine clothing and shoes and wearing that in private, but it was quite a while before she was doing that in more public contexts. I didn't know what being gender-queer was going to look like in the future for Noah. I was figuring that it could be a private thing. It may have been a bit of denial for several months. Then I met [Rev.] Katie [Hays] for coffee, and we talked some about Noah, and she said, "I think this is going to go further than you expect. I don't think this is the end. There's going to be more."

Her college graduation was coming up, spring 2017, and we didn't know who all was coming to graduation. My parents said they were coming, and we still hadn't gotten around to telling them about Noah. So I composed a two-page letter trying to explain what gender-queer is to my eighty-something-year-old parents, and I sent it in the mail because they don't really do email. I didn't hear anything back from them.

I called them the night before graduation. My mother answered the phone, and I said, "Hey, did you all get the letter I sent earlier this week?" And my mother said, "Yeah. Where are we supposed to meet you on campus for graduation?" And then she hands the phone off to my dad, and he says, "Hey, you tell Noah no worries. Tell him . . . tell Noah we love him. You know, this is a new world, a changing world, and we've got to learn to make our way in it."

So they came and sat with us at graduation. Afterwards we went out to eat. Noah was wearing a black dress and high heels and amazing makeup. After dinner, we were out in the parking lot, and my dad says to Noah, "You know, this is not going to be an easy road for you, but I'm confident that you're going to be all right. You can handle it. You can do it."

Karen

Noah informed us one by one. I was like, "Okay. Now what do you want for dinner?" It didn't disturb me at all. Her sister's response was, "Well, that just gives me more to love."

I didn't spend a lot of time thinking about where it might be going. I just said, "I accept you, I accept this. There's no problem with me. Carry on. I'm good." I can't explain that. It's just that I love my kids, and I love them for who they are. I have always told them, "Be who you are, not who you think I think I should be. Be yourself," because I didn't get that choice. I was told who I was, and I'd better toe the line. And I was dead set against being that kind of a parent.

I lived in fear of my dad for sixty of my sixty-one years. I was afraid of crossing the line in any area, because he would take it out on me. He would scream at me. He was very emotionally abusive to the family. And his reputation in the church was more important than his kids.

Over the last twenty years, my dad was hospitalized a lot. I would take care of him. I would work all day in Fort Worth, then drive over to Dallas, and I'd stay the night shift at the hospital so my mother could go home and sleep. And then she'd come back in the morning, and I'd drive back and teach all day. And then do it again, and do it again.

Then when my mother was coming out of rehab after her major stroke, my dad said, "I want you to quit your job and come be her caretaker." I said, "Excuse me? I can't do that." "Why not?" he said.

I put off telling my dad about Noah's gender identity until the last possible moment, because of the feared reaction, which was absolutely right on. It was horrible. J. [Noah's sister] was getting married a year after Noah's graduation in May 2018.

Kurt

Even though her mother was, by that time, living in assisted living and had speech problems, they insisted they were coming to J.'s wedding. So we said, "Okay, they're coming to the wedding. We've got . . ."

Karen

"Time's run out. They've got to know."

Kurt

I sent basically the same two-page letter I'd sent my parents, with a little bit of updating about what Noah had done in the year just past.

Karen

Then my dad called me, and he screamed at me for almost twelve minutes. My father, screaming. Kurt could hear it. It wasn't even on speakerphone. He's screaming, blaming me. "How can this be? How can you let this happen? This goes against everything I've preached for fifty years," and just on and on and on. I finally cut him off. I said, "You know what? We've got a wedding tomorrow. I've got to go."

Kurt

He said, "We're coming to the wedding, but I'm going to keep my distance from Noah."

Karen

It was as bad as we anticipated—or even worse.

Kurt

So Noah and Rory came to the wedding at just the last minute before it started, and they sat in the very back row.

Karen

They texted and said, "Where are they [Noah's grandparents] sitting?" They sat as far away as they could get. And Noah sat there hiding behind her hair. Remembering what happened makes me very angry and very defensive and protective. How dare grandparents act like that? How dare my father be that way toward his grandchild? And so I cut off communication with him.

Kurt

A couple weeks later, her dad calls and leaves a voicemail saying, "Why aren't you returning my calls?"

Karen

Two weeks after the wedding, my brother calls me. He says, "You need to call Dad. He's all upset. He says he's been cast out of the family circle." And I said, "Oh, no. That's not it at all." And I explained to my brother, and he's like, "Well, I understand. I get it. But you need to—" I said, "No. I'm not going to call him. This is on him. He owes me an apology. He cast us out. If he's going to draw the line and make us choose, I'm standing with Noah. There's no way I would not."

I don't know what my siblings' reaction to Noah was. I really don't. I don't even know how we told them. I don't remember. It was not as traumatic as it was with my parents. I wasn't really worried about what their reactions would be. I could not care less what their reactions were, really.

My mother I don't think ever knew, because the last thing my father ever said to me was a threat: "Don't you ever do anything to upset my wife." I don't know how he explained my absence over the past years. She had numerous strokes, and the big one affected her speech center, and she couldn't read anymore. There was no way to have a meaningful conversation with her.

My father never made amends. I didn't speak to him or see him again after J.'s wedding. Later, when Dad was sick again, people from church would call and say, "Your dad is in really rough shape. He checked himself into the hospital," and I just ignored it. I would not tolerate this attitude toward my child. Because if he was going to draw a line, then I was going to stand with Noah. No question. Absolutely none. That's my kid. I'm a mama bear. Believe me. Don't cross me about my kids.

Kurt

There was another email and voicemail. This was about a month after the wedding. He said, "I haven't had time to think back through the conversation about what might have offended," or something like that. And "I don't think I should be cast out of the family circle because of my convictions about Noah's lifestyle," or something like that. Or "Noah's choices," or whatever. And, "I continue to pray for Noah every day, and I don't blame you, Karen." So after a couple months, we worked on a letter to him.

Karen

It's a most epic letter.

Kurt

It was about eleven or twelve points or something, in paragraphs. We showed it to some people to get their reaction to it before we sent it off. Katie read it and said, "You know, this is the most amazing email I've ever read. I wish everybody at Galileo could advocate for themselves or their loved ones like you're doing, speaking the truth in love." I sent that, and her dad sent back about twelve lines and attempted an apology.

I wrote back to him and said, "Well, I suppose that's a first step. There's still a lot that needs to be said and questions that need to be answered." He did acknowledge sorrow for the pain. He said, "I make no excuses, but I can't promise that something like this will never happen again, because it might. At my age and with my nature, I can't guarantee that it won't happen again."

One thing I asked in the longer letter was, is Noah going to be welcome at family gatherings, holiday gatherings, or what? You talk about wanting to keep your distance, and yet you say, "I understand your feelings of wanting to stand with Noah." So I said,

"Well, if it's okay for us to continue to associate with Noah, why is it different for you?"

But in his short apology letter, he didn't say anything about Noah. He didn't answer any questions about how he planned to relate to Noah in the future, whether Noah would be welcome there at Christmas or Thanksgiving or birthdays. He didn't touch on that at all. I had said, in my letter, that the graduation and the wedding or whatever, those occasions are not the time for discussion and debate about Noah being gender-queer. I said, "I know this is a hard thing to wrap your mind around. This is my best effort to explain this right now, but there may be an occasion in the future when we can talk about it some more." And we did say we're not going anywhere that Noah's not welcome. If you don't indicate that Noah is welcome to come to your home or to our family get-togethers, don't expect us to show up for those.

Karen

I teach at a private Christian school. They absolutely do not affirm any of this. I have to kind of hide. But I stay there because there are lots of kids there who are on the rainbow. There are. Whether the administration acknowledges it or not, the kids need somebody safe. And they know I'm it. We don't ever have to bring it up. They know they've got somebody who loves them for who they are, regardless of anything else. I feel that's important, to be there for that.

There will come a time when I am done with it, because it's not easy to work for a place that is not affirming of my child. When Noah started posting pictures on Facebook, the profile pictures of her in a dress, the band director caught me in the mail room one day and said, "So, what do you think about this, Noah wearing dresses?" I said, "I love my child for who they are, and Noah is not a topic for discussion here. Ever." Nobody's brought it up since. But I feel strongly that all kids need to know somebody is in

their corner, and it doesn't matter how they identify, that they are
worthy of acceptance.

Kurt

I've been teaching Sunday school for fifteen years or so at the
church where Noah was raised. I think I have a role there. An elder's son came out as gay. He asked me, what do I think about that,
and I said, "Well, let me give you a reading list." He appreciated
that, and he did a lot of reading. He told me later, "You really made
a big difference for me. You were a lifesaver, and you opened up
my mind to a different way of thinking."

I've had some other parents at the church whose kids have
come out as bi or gay or whatever. Or just other people who are
wrestling with doubts or questions about their traditional reading
of the Bible in general.

Talking to other parents about their child coming out, I say
I have to admit I can't understand fully, can't get inside of Noah
and see and feel what she sees and feels and knows. I've got to trust
that she knows herself better than anyone else. I think we're coming to learn that sexuality and gender are a lot more complicated
than we've known. And you can be sure that people don't come
to this realization about themselves easily or casually. They don't
wake up one day and say, "Oh, I think I'll be trans; that looks like
it might be fun or joyful."

Karen

You went to see my dad in hospice before he died.

Kurt

Yeah. I thought, "Maybe I should go. I'd like to go see him," just to
see what his situation was. Was there any opportunity for there

being a better, more satisfying ending to this? I texted Karen and said, "I'm thinking of going over there. But I won't if you object." She said, "You do what you need to do."

I was at Galileo. I left right after communion. At that point I was all choked up and sobbing. I told Katie what I was going to do and she gave me a hug and sent me on. But when I got there, he was asleep. I said his name a couple of times. He woke up and greeted me like he always did: "Hey, B. [Kurt's last name]. What's going on?"

He asked about Noah: "How's Noah doing?" And I said, "Well, you know, she got married at the end of July." And he said, "Well, I hope everything works out for them." It came time to go, and he said "Well, let's let me pray." And he said, "Lord, bless all the B. family," and then a long pause, and, "In Jesus' name, amen."

Karen

I did not go see him. I am at peace with how I've done everything. I am. I was there for uncountable hours of care and enduring tirades. And I just took it. But if you're going to make me choose, I'm with Noah.

"FAMILY IS BULLSHIT"

Noah (she/her)

Noah (she/her) is in her twenties. She recently graduated from college and even more recently married Rory (they/them), whose story is told elsewhere in this book. Noah is the child of Kurt (he/him) and Karen (she/her) and the child-in-law of Jackie (she/her), whose stories are also included in this book.

Noah is gender-queer, describing herself as "mostly woman, but a little bit not." She didn't really worry whether her immediate family of origin would be supportive of her gender identity, but she and her parents worried together about Noah's grandparents. For a while she avoided confrontation by staying away from family gatherings. In an extended family that was not really close, it did not seem like much of a loss.

Noah describes the fear that accompanies her gender identity, which can't be hidden unless she chooses to present inauthentically—a compromise she is not willing to make. "That kind of peace is not important to me," she says, implying that any peace that requires her to remain hidden from the rest of us is not really peace at all.

MY IMMEDIATE FAMILY used to go on camping trips all the time, mostly to the American Southwest, and we'd do a lot of hiking. There's a parallel between the hiking trips that we would take and the way my family of origin walked alongside me when I came out.

Gender-queer was the first term I had that sounded right to me, about myself. I've stuck with it. For some people it might mean I'm not man and I'm not woman. But for me, I'm mostly woman. I'm mostly woman, but a little bit not. That's why I chose that term. People will identify with the same terms for different reasons, and it might mean something different to them than it does for another person. There are some people who are functionally pretty much the same as me, but would choose *nonbinary* instead of *gender-queer.*

The first person I came out to within my immediate family was my sister. After I kind of explained who I am, and a little bit of my experience, and where I was at that particular point, I asked her, "Am I still your brother?" (At that point I was still using masculine pronouns.) Her response was, "Well, yeah. You're just more you than you were before." I think that's a very poignant way to look at it. That was wonderful.

Pretty soon after, I came out to my mom. I don't remember the particulars of that conversation. My mom is one of those parents who is over-the-top supportive. She is effusive in her expressions of love for her children and her desire for us to be whoever we are. She wants us to know that she does not expect us to fulfill any expectations that anybody has for us. So yes, I know that's how she reacted.

I was a little nervous about coming out to my dad. Not because I didn't think he'd be supportive, but it's harder for him and me to have intense, deeply emotional conversations. We're a little bit less connected that way. So I told him last. He was supportive and encouraging. Being the scholar that he is, he started reading a whole bunch of things. The things he cares about, and the people he cares about, he reads about, to help him understand. That's how he showed support and love for me.

In terms of extended family, the only person that I told soon after I came out to my immediate family was my cousin. She was supportive and affirming, and five minutes later she was rambling about *Hamilton*. She rolled with it.

But before I came out to anybody in my family, the first person I told was actually my ex-girlfriend. Our relationship had lasted like three weeks, and then we remained friends. I'd been experimenting with wearing femme clothes in the privacy of my dorm room. She was talking about some serious stuff with her family. And I thought, *You know what? Maybe I should start opening up about this.* Since we had already kind of been talking about some really serious personal topics, I came out to her.

She was super supportive. She said, "You should also tell other people. Don't keep this to yourself, because I can tell that it's hurting you to have this bottled up." So the next day I told another one of my friends. We were both already super pro-LGBTQ+ rights, and we were both feminists, so I already knew that she would be supportive.

I came out to [Rev.] Katie [Hays] the next day. She was supportive. So by virtue of already being a social-justice-minded person, an advocate, I already had a support system built up before I even knew that I was gender-queer, before I knew that I had something to come out about. I came out to a whole bunch of people really, really quickly, and it was nothing but affirmation from anybody that I told.

Galileo Church was a place where all three of the things that mean the most to me could coexist: faith, music, and identity. I don't have to choose which parts of me I want to be open about or to hide. I don't have to check my brain at the door. I don't have to check my cello at the door, like I did in the Church of Christ I was raised in. And I don't have to check my identity at the door.

But it was still a big deal for me to come out at Galileo, because the thing about gender identity is that it has implications for your appearance. If you're a gay guy, you can just not talk about your boyfriend. Once I put on a dress, I've kind of decided, *Okay, until I change my clothes somewhere, I'm out of the closet.*

Before I came out to Galileo Church as a whole, I came out to my G-group [part of Galileo Church's small group infrastructure]. The G-group became a safe space for me to experiment with what it's like to wear femme clothes, dresses and stuff like that, around people. It was a smaller, private setting where confidentiality and trust were guaranteed. I trusted that they would treat me the way I wanted to be treated, and they weren't going to do anything to endanger me. It was so important for me to have that space.

So I would come to G-group with a duffel bag with a dress packed in it, change once I got there, then change back out before going back to school. Later I started doing that in worship too. It took a lot longer before I could go about in the rest of the world as who I am.

I was scared, scared of the attention, not because I thought it'd be bad, but just because I didn't want it. I didn't feel ready to deal with the natural attention that such a big change in my appearance was going to get. Eventually I prepared myself for that, and there was a lot of attention, but I was okay with it. It doesn't mean it was easy or that I particularly liked every single aspect of coming out, but it was worth it.

I can't really think of anything that surprised me about coming out. I knew it was going to be difficult. I knew Galileo would be affirming of me. I knew my family would be affirming of me—at least my immediate family would be affirming of me. I guess the one thing that would qualify as a surprise is that my dad's parents are cool with it. The way we navigated it with them, being unsure, was basically for a while I stopped going to extended family functions. To be honest, independent of affirmation or nonaffirmation of queer people, I don't really enjoy my extended family that much.

And I had the excuse of college—working on a paper, whatever, can't go. But then my college graduation was coming up. My grandma and grandpa, my dad's parents, wanted to be there, and

I was obviously going to be wearing a dress and whatnot. I asked my dad to write a letter to them, kind of coming out to them on my behalf. That wasn't a conversation I felt comfortable having, because we did not know how they were going to react. They're not the most religious people, but they're also east Texans. So, you know.

My dad wrote this letter kind of explaining my gender identity, all that kind of stuff, and sent it to his father. We didn't get a response from them, so Dad called and said, "Hey, did you get that letter?" And Grandma was like, "Oh, yeah, we got it. Tell Noah everything's all good. Everything's fine. You know, we love Noah and we'll keep loving him."

They still fuck up our pronouns, mine and Rory's, but it's so much different when you know there's a baseline of affirmation. When someone who you know is cool with your identity is messing up your pronouns, it is a lot different than when someone who's not cool with your identity messes up pronouns. I'm a lot more forgiving of my dad's parents than of Rory's grandparents, who are nonaffirming. Sometimes they've even intentionally messed up my pronouns. I have a high standard. Rory's grandparents have to do so much more for me to trust them than my grandparents.

I didn't think that the rest of my extended family would be okay with it, and that is definitely the case with my mom's parents. They are not okay at all with it. Grandpa is a Church of Christ pastor, retired pastor, super conservative. We knew there wasn't a question that they would be nonaffirming if they found out, and so again I stopped going to extended family gatherings.

There was one Christmas a few years ago that it looked like we were going to have to tell them something, but then Mom got pneumonia or something like that, so we had to skip Christmas with the family. It sucks that she got pneumonia, but I was glad to avoid that confrontation. I wasn't about to dress neutrally to avoid a confrontation, because I'm done with that. I did that for the first twenty years of my life, and I'm not about to go back and do it again. That kind of peace is not important to me.

But then my sister got married, and we knew we were going to have to tell them. I said to my parents, "Look, I'm showing up to this wedding in a dress. I would like for you all to tell them beforehand. I'm not having that conversation with them. You all do what you want."

Dad sent pretty much the same letter he had sent his father. My mom got a phone call from her dad, and he was livid. He was screaming at her. Mom hasn't spoken to him since. Neither have I, obviously. I don't really have use for people who aren't affirming. I had never really liked them. And I'm not going to take shit from people that I don't really. . . . There's no reason to. Just because my mom is their kid, is that a reason for me to accept things from them that I wouldn't accept from other people? I've always had a "family is bullshit" mentality. Like, if they're going to be loving, okay. Cool. Awesome. That's great. If they're not going to be loving, well, fuck 'em. They're useless to me. That didn't feel like a loss to me, because I already knew that I had lost them. Even before that, they knew that they had lost me. I just knew that was the case.

They were at J.'s wedding, and I was still scared, and Rory and I just sat in the back, and I avoided any interaction with my grandparents. It sucked, but being authentic and avoiding my grandparents was better than not avoiding my grandparents and being inauthentic.

I'm scared more than you might think. When one person messes up my pronouns, even if I know they love me, and there's really no issue of my safety, my brain still jumps. There's a whole bunch of stuff to think about, like, *Okay, do I correct them? How do I correct them? How are they going to react if I do?* There are so many things that even for somebody you're close to, there's a long list that your brain automatically goes through. You never know when that's going to happen, so you've always got to be ready to decide and choose the best way to react, in a split second.

When I'm going out shopping, just grocery shopping, there's so much to think about. Most people think, *Okay, am I wearing clothes? Good. Do I need to brush my hair?* But for me, it's like, Number one, how much work do I want to do to get ready before going out? Do I have time, if I feel like shaving my face? Or shaving my legs? And if I don't, then I might not dress as femme as I prefer to, because of the contrast in expectations, societally speaking. I have to consider, how self-confident am I feeling today? When people look at me weird or stare at me, do I feel prepared to handle that today? All those kinds of considerations come into play every single time that I leave the house.

I know it's going to be okay. I have found someone who loves me. I don't know if there's anything I'd do differently, looking back. Okay, I lost a couple friends when I came out. There was some hard stuff. But the people I gained and the things it did for my own health and life have been absolutely worth it. Absolutely.

REFLECTIONS
· AND ·
CONCLUSIONS

A ROAD MAP WITH A DESTINATION FOR EVERYONE

The Social Scientist's Reflections

Susan A. Chiasson

When you are faced with a task—in this case, coming out to your family of origin—that could go well, go wrong, or go very, *very* wrong, it makes sense to look for guidance from those who have already done it and who find themselves still standing and even flourishing. When we asked some of our friends at Galileo what it was like, what worked, and what didn't, their answers varied widely, of course. The only testimony you can give is what happened to *you*, in *your* life. But it's my work to look for commonalities, threads that run through and tie together diverse experiences. Here I'll summarize and discuss what I learned from my friends, hoping to outline a road map of sorts, showing what can happen along the way and what one could do to prepare and make it through.

Before going further, let me note several limitations on my work. (1) This is a small sample, not a definitive survey; a beginning, not a conclusion. (2) I'm not an expert in queer studies, and I have no theories I'm trying to squeeze these accounts into. (3) I'm not truly objective, as I said in my introduction; I refer to the people I talked to as *friends*, not respondents, because that's what they are: friends of mine and of Galileo Church. (4) While we've distilled each story to fit into these pages, I'm drawing upon each entire conversation. I can recall what it was like to hear someone's voice break, or laugh uproariously, or struggle to express a difficult thought. If you can't hear the same in the narratives you've just read, you might have to trust me for some of the nuance.

I first asked each person (or couple), "What was it like to come out?" and I asked them to look at an array of photos and to choose, quickly, the picture that captured that experience best. No one had trouble selecting a picture. All but one person chose pictures that were dark, confusing, or messy. When I asked them to talk about what their pictures meant to them, no one hesitated. Everyone had a story ready to go. As Leanne explained to me, *As a queer person, one of the first things you share when you meet a new queer person is, "What is your coming-out story?"* Rory described how developing and telling their story made their new identity real to them, comparing it to joining a secret club: *The more people that I told before I got to my family of origin, the more real it felt. It feels strange the first time you claim that as your own. But once I had told it a couple of times, it started to feel like my own story.*

Having "my own story" helped each of our friends organize their experience and make sense of it. Here I have followed their lead, organizing my discussion around four challenges they all dealt with: (1) coming to terms with your queer identity; (2) deciding to come out; (3) preparing for coming out; and (4) recalibrating family relationships afterward.

In my final section, I'll take a step back to appreciate where our friends are taking us with this road map for coming out to your family of origin. They describe what you might encounter along the way, suggesting resources and strategies for each challenge. They evoke a destination that makes rough travel worth the struggle. It turns out they've given us a road map that could guide not only queer people, their families, and their allies; but also anyone else who hopes for the fairness and freedom required for shalom.

Challenge 1: Coming to Terms with Your Queer Identity

In the stories our friends told, the starting point of coming out is *before* the actual moment of saying it to someone you love for the first time. It's a period where a queer person realizes they're queer *and* they live in a society where a lot of people believe queer is wrong. In this time, they figure out how to resolve that conflict, how to come to terms with who they are and whether to come out. This is how our friends talked about these tasks.

New Fact: "I'm Different, I'm Queer"

There's Kyra, who explained, *I've always been weird.... I've always been different, and [my extended family] never liked that I didn't fit in.* Leanne knew she was different in high school because she didn't want to date. Then at a college dance, she had a lightbulb moment: *Sure enough, there were people of the same sex dancing together, and it just clicked right there: that was me! I still didn't know what it was, but I quickly figured it out. That was how I was different.*

Feeling different is a clue, and so is acting differently. Cole *felt* different as a teenager, but it was the search for male underwear models he left on the family computer that prompted his parents to ask him if he was gay. He wasn't ready to come out: *I said, "Maybe I'm bisexual. I don't know what I am."* But he knew he was different. Evelyn had a relationship before she had the words for her identity: *I met a girl in high school who was my best friend, and it became an intimate relationship, and then we became girlfriends, and then we were like very closeted. And we didn't even know what gay meant.* Ava echoed Evelyn's point about feelings preceding vocabulary: *I came out when I was seventeen. I knew earlier, but I didn't have words for it. But I knew. When I was seventeen, I confided in a camp counselor.*

Realization can be slow. Marion said, *I realized I was gay in 2003 when I fell in love with my best friend*—after she'd been married to a man, had kids, and divorced. Rory and Noah both had a period of "I don't feel like everyone else seems to be feeling" before they could clearly see themselves.

Whether realization was instantaneous or over time, it was based on feelings and actions, not a rational thought process. No one said, "I chose . . ." or "I decided. . . ." Kurt, Noah's dad, made this point when he said, talking about Noah: *You can be sure that people don't come to this realization about themselves easily or casually. They don't wake up one day and say, "Oh, I think I'll be trans; that looks like it might be fun or joyful."* Science tells us that a lot of factors, some biological, some social/cultural, contribute to a person's gender identity and sexual orientation. Free choice is not one of those factors. In our friends' stories, you don't think your way to being queer, you feel and act your way to it, listening to what your body and heart tell you.

But "Queer Is Wrong"

There's another reason to believe that no one chooses to be queer: many people disapprove of it. Leanne lamented that she would have liked to have children, but it was not acceptable, she thought, when she came out in the '80s. Marion described how her parents talked about gay people: *I've heard Daddy say things. I have heard Mama, more than once, if there's somebody who's not married, usually a guy who's not married for a long, long time, she'll be talking to another lady in the church her age and she'll say, "Do you think he's . . . ?" and there's a pause, just dead space. "Do you think he's . . . ?"* It's easy to see why Marion concluded, *Well shit, I don't want them talking about me like that.*

Resolving "I'm Queer" and "Queer Is Wrong"

Psychological theory and research tell us that when people are confronted with a new fact at odds with their existing beliefs, they feel discomfort and try to fix it. One resolution is to assimilate the new fact into existing beliefs: "Oh, it's not so different from how I think about *x* anyway." Another is more like anti-resolution, a choice to ignore, deny, or simply live with the discomfort for a while, perhaps hoping that it will disappear on its own. A third option is adapting beliefs to encompass new facts: "I now see that I was wrong about *x*; let me change what I think."

"Queer is wrong," as our friends encountered it, was based on two objections, one religious ("It's a sin") and the other biological ("It's unnatural"). Our friends all found ways to question and reject those beliefs, demonstrating how to adapt to these new facts. From the beginning, coming out asks a queer person to reconsider and reject the cisgender-heterocentric status quo.

Religious Objections

Our friends were familiar with church disapproval. Kyra said about her extended family, *Everyone blamed my parents for not making us Christian enough to not be gay.* Leanne explained how she knew she couldn't come out: *You come out of that fundamentalist, evangelical background, and you just know. It's preached about from the pulpits.* Rory, Noah, Ava, and Marion were also aware that the evangelical churches they were raised in condemned being queer.

In two instances, churches harmed our friends. Jake came out to his girlfriend, who told her parents, who told church elders. They all encouraged him to try conversion therapy, which he did for six or seven months. It turns out, Jake said, *Ex-gay therapy is bullshit.* But he spent another year and half trying not to be gay and found it exhausting. Cole's parents, thinking they were helping him with depression, sent him to a religious counselor—who broke confidentiality by telling Cole's youth pastor he was wrestling with his sexual orientation. The youth pastor subsequently gave an anti-gay sermon and told the confused kids, "I know that somebody here is dealing with this." Cole reflected, *I felt like I couldn't trust, really trust, leaders in the church.*

Our friends combatted religious objections with a combination of education and intuition. Ava and Jake explained how educating themselves helped. Ava read about different religions, including Chinese philosophy and Taoism: *All of this has to do with being peaceful with where you are, and there's always this sense about you that you have to accept yourself.* Jake's struggles with religious strictures ended when he discovered the Gay Christian Network (a nonprofit now called Q Christian Fellowship), which provided him with theological answers in a supportive community.

Others intuited that institutional religion had missed the boat. Remembering a queer Christian conference she attended, Marion exclaimed: *There were all these books . . . meant to convince you that even though you're gay, God still loves you. What the hell? I don't need all these books. God and I are fine.* Leanne had an intuition that the church was wrong about her going to hell: *I had this innate sense that the church was wrong about this. I wasn't going to hell even before I was baptized, because if you say God made everything, then God made me. How can I go to hell?* Jake didn't begin with an innate sense that the church was wrong, but his efforts to work through what it meant for him to be gay and Christian led to a revelation that God fully accepted him as gay. *The one thing that holds me to my faith is that I'm queer. This is how I connect with God. Because we have a very queer God, and I'm a very queer man.*

Biological Objections

Another objection to queerness is that it's unnatural or disgusting. When Evelyn's parents discovered she was gay, her mom gave vent to this objection: *I remember seeing my mom slouched on the bathroom floor just sobbing, sobbing, saying every time she thinks of us together it makes her want to vomit.* Jake's mom, not knowing one of her children was gay, explained to her kids that homosexuality is abnormal, a mental illness. Jake knew he was gay at thirteen, but once he heard his mom's position, he resolved to never tell anybody—and didn't for fifteen years.

As with religious objections, our friends relied on education and intuition to reject this objection. Kyra advocates learning as much as possible about gender and sexuality: *No one can make me doubt the choices I've made, because I have made them with education. . . . We read all these toxic, horrible theories about trans people. But science supports trans people.* Ava was encouraged by a licensed professional counselor to read up on being gay: *I went to [the] library and there was a section for all the gay literature. It had the letters HQ before everything and I laughed: homosexual, queer. . . . I read everything I could find . . . and that was helpful to me, just learning what I could.* That, plus college classes on human sexuality, gave Ava a broader perspective.

Ava also had an intuition she was fine, rejecting a counselor who tried to talk her out of her identity: *Honestly, I thought he was full of shit. . . . I didn't have the words for that, but that was my attitude because I was just kind of figuring out this is who I am.* Evelyn had that certainty in her gut as well: *Even though at the time I probably couldn't process that or think about that logically, all I knew was what felt good and I had to get away from what felt bad.* Intuition, trusting what your body tells you, played a big part in our friends' realization they were different in the first place, and it continued to inform them that the problem wasn't them but a mistaken belief about being queer.

Coming to terms with being queer when others disapprove takes time, often years. As Evelyn said of her family of origin, *It took time, but it got easier and easier.* Ava said that after several years, she woke up one morning, and voilà: *I just wasn't worried about being gay. It just wasn't on my mind, "Am I saved?," all of that, it just was gone.* Cole, who stayed in the closet for a few years, noted that changes in his life and in society over those years encouraged him to come out: *I had a great network of friends. "Born This Way" had just come out. It was just like this bubble burst. I was finally, like, "It's okay to be gay!"*

Education, intuition, and time guided our friends in rejecting the belief that queer is wrong. Cole summed up his struggle: *It was more about me accepting myself.* One way or another, our friends were able to reach a place of *I'm queer and queer is fine.* They began to tell the story of who they were to themselves and to others. The next challenge was deciding whether to come out to their family of origin, a decision that required weighing self-protection against self-expression.

Challenge 2: Deciding to Come Out: Self-Protection versus Self-Expression

Each of our friends had reasons for their decision to come out (or not), and when, and how widely, and they are the best judges of what worked for their situations. Their reasons fall roughly into two categories: protecting themselves and expressing themselves.

"I Owe It to Myself to Protect Myself (Not Tell)"

For Leanne and Marion, who are in their fifties, the decision was made years ago, in a different time. Marion addressed generational differences: *For people who are my age, a lot of us may still be secretive. . . . It's almost at the DNA level to keep it private.* Leanne was sure her religious family would reject her: *You've heard the stories of gay people who've come out to their evangelical family members and are kicked out of their houses.* For Marion, it was a combination of her family and social pressures. *Mama'd probably cry, Daddy'd probably cry,* and also, *I don't know that I would have lost my job as a teacher, but nobody would have wanted their kid in my class had they known.* Recently, they've both come out to select members of their families of origin.

Staying safe concerned several of our friends, who on occasion fear for their physical safety. Ava had a neighbor who threatened to shoot her and her girlfriend; Noah has been catcalled by frat boys; Kyra worries about looking different in public; and Leanne noted that she thinks twice before she holds her wife's hand in public. Not all these instances made it into the distilled narratives, as we focused narrowly on relational dynamics within families of origin. I mention them here to underscore that a concern for safety is not only about fearing someone will say something derogatory. It's a fear for whether that verbal abuse is an opening for a more serious threat. Statistics about violence against the LBGTQ+ community confirm the validity of this concern. Neve, who hovered around her wife Kyra's interview, captured the push and pull of "gotta come out" versus "gotta be safe": *There's a wealth of people waiting for you in this life you're scared to live.*

"I Owe It to Myself to Express Myself (Tell)"

Some friends made the conscious decision to come out on their own, careful timetable in order to avoid hurting themselves. After Noah told a close friend that she was queer, the friend urged her to tell others, saying, *"Don't keep this to yourself, because I can tell that it's hurting you to have this bottled up."* Noah told another friend the next day, and the cascade continued. Kyra knew Neve had to come out for her own good, noting that *the relief of having come out and not keeping this a secret anymore was so much better.*

Sometimes coming out is a way to avoid hurting others. Leanne had decided not to come out to her family of origin, but on reflection she discerned that hiding had hurt her family relationships: *Everyone knows you're gay. . . . You're really damaging the relationships you want to save.*

Our friends talked about other reasons to come out, too. For Jake, it was about his relationship to God: *I got to this point where I couldn't say that I was following God and* not *come out—which was the most terrifying realization I've ever come to.* For Kyra, it was about fighting stigma and normalizing queer identity: *Trans people need visibility. We need people to see.* Leanne echoes that point when she says, *If you hide in the closet, you're sending the message that there's some shame associated with who you are and what you are. . . . If you come out of the closet, you show that there is no shame in who you are.*

Practice Makes Comfortable

Before coming out to their families of origin, though, many of our friends did practice runs with strangers, acquaintances, or friends. Noah told a friend first, as did Kyra and Neve. Ava told a camp counselor first. When Marion gave voice to her identity, she did so to strangers at a celebration of the Supreme Court's ruling on gay marriage, held in a town forty-five minutes away from her home, adding that she knew this was safe place: *I told a couple strangers. Not family.* Rory first told their story to people outside their family as well. When Cole felt he was getting ready to come out to his family, he turned first to his network of gay friends: *I talked to one of them and asked for advice.*

Challenge 3:
Preparing for Coming Out to Your Family of Origin

So far, I've described two parts of the coming-out process: discovering and coming to terms with your queer identity and deciding to come out. Next come two more challenges—preparing to come out to your family and reckoning with the aftermath.

I'm describing these as though they go in order, 1–2–3, but since you've read the narratives, you know it's not that neat. Coming to terms can take years, even after you've come out and reckoned with your family.

For the sake of simplicity, let's look at another part, the actual coming out, as if it neatly comes next. Having accepted your queer self, you now ask your family of origin to accept your queer self as well. What can you expect? Leanne advised, *You have to be prepared that things could go really badly for you. But they might also be fine.* So how can you prepare for an outcome you can't predict?

As I contemplated and analyzed our friends' accounts, I saw two objectives, or maybe hopes: to have your family respond with respect and warm embrace, and to be still standing and whole no matter how your family responds. The experiences of our friends suggest at least the following:

- you can't control your family's response;
- it pays to be familiar with your family's track record on being open and unbiased, on being able to talk calmly about tough topics, and on expressing unconditional love; and
- you can take actions to protect yourself.

You Can't Control Your Family's Response

Both Kyra and Jake had control over the *when* and *where* and *who* of coming out, with different responses from their various family members. Kyra and Neve planned carefully because they were sure that, however well Kyra's parents (Daniel and Kellie) took the news, the extended family would react bigly and badly. (They were not wrong.) So Kyra told Daniel, alone, and asked him to tell Kellie, and relied on both of them to tell the extended family. Doing so spared them the initial fireworks when the extended family learned that Neve was a trans woman, and Kellie and Daniel continue to be a buffer between their daughter and daughter-in-law and Kellie's extended family.

Jake also controlled his coming out to the point where he chose to pass up an opportunity to tell his whole family, together for a holiday, because he decided he didn't want to disrupt the celebration. When he told them later, individually, responses were all over the map. He told his youngest sister first, thinking she'd be a safe audience, and it seemed to go well. As he told others, he got mixed reactions: his sisters seemed sometimes okay, sometimes not, but also disappointingly uninterested in something that was central to his identity. His younger brother told him he was sinning. His father, a libertarian, while okay with Jake's orientation, offered little more than a recommendation that he join the Log Cabin Republicans. Only his older half-brother gave warm support and offers of tangible help, should Jake need it.

Evelyn, Ava, and Rory came out with little control over the moment. Evelyn's parents confronted her when she had her girlfriend over, and she was catapulted into coming out, unprepared for the volcanic negative response from her parents. Ava's mom found out when she looked at a phone bill and saw calls to a number she didn't recognize. She asked Ava for an explanation, and Ava disclosed the truth; her mom collapsed and called her husband to come home right away. As Ava says, *That was the start of some really difficult things with my mom and some beautiful things with my father,* as her dad hugged her and assured her of his love.

As for Rory, they didn't intend to tell their mother when they did, but found themself becoming psychically and physically exhausted by remaining hidden at a holiday event with extended family, and they ended up blurting it out in the car to their mom: *She was very kind.* (Rory and Jackie, her mom, both agree it was a rocky experience saved by love.)

All these experiences underscore that control over the circumstances of coming out does not guarantee welcome from your family of origin. Other factors are also at work, having to do with how your family has always acted.

Realistically Assess Your Family's Track Record on Openness/ Bias, Talking Calmly, and Unconditional Love

As I considered these accounts of our friends' actual coming-out moments, I saw that the prior capacity of the family of origin to handle new and disruptive information made a difference. I was drawn to three capacities in particular: being open-minded, being able to talk about tough issues calmly, and being willing to express unconditional love. Assessing your family's capacities can help you anticipate how coming out will go. Channeling Scotty from *Star Trek*, ask yourself, *Is the ship built to take this kind of speed?*

This assessment has two parts, both tricky: making the assessment itself, and knowing whether you're actually right in your assessment. Both parts are tricky because we take for granted how our families work and rarely step back and analyze their ways. Also, a family can pay lip service to one thing and do another. It's tricky to do and tricky to get right, but those who were intentional in doing this had fewer surprises.

Openness/Bias

First, how does your family talk about queer people? About marginalized people in general? Kellie was sure that her family would erupt at Kyra and Neve's news, and they did. As Kyra observed, one tip-off was the family's response to the Supreme Court ruling on gay marriage: *My family decides to hold a prayer about that. . . . Everyone holds hands, because we're all so scared, because now gay people can get married.* Marion relied on talk she had heard and action she had witnessed when she decided to come out to her daughter: *I felt like it would be a safe experience. . . . I'd seen how she acted with her friends who were gay. I'd seen her stand up to my daddy when he said something derogatory about one of her best friends who's a gay guy.*

But surprises can happen. Jackie mistook a repeated declaration by her husband and herself that "We will always love our children, no matter what" for openness. Looking back, she saw clues to bias that she didn't see at the time, leading her to sum this situation up as finally *smelling the shit that was always there.*

By contrast, Cole was sure his family was anti-gay because they snarked about characters and celebrities in TV shows like *Will & Grace* and *Queer Eye*. When they embraced him, and he had more discussions with them, he realized that his family had a long track record of supporting gay rights and walking away from bigots.

Often people use a proxy measure for openness and bias, like religiosity or political leanings. But those aren't necessarily reliable predictors. Noah's paternal grandfather fits the profile of evangelical Christian and right-wing Republican, and he accepts his young relative unreservedly. Cole worried what his religious grandfather might think of him, but his grandfather assured him that his experience as a preacher had not only clued him in to the reality that some men are attracted to men but had also made him sympathetic to their suffering. Then his grandfather, unprompted by Cole, began to argue that the Bible, taken in context, is not anti-queer. Cole reacted with surprise and relief: *I took a big breath after he said that.* "Wow, you get it, Grandpa." Likewise, Kurt's dad reassured Kurt that he got the big picture, saying, *This is a new world, a changing world, and we've got to learn to make our way in it.*

Talking Calmly about Tough Topics

Second, has your family of origin shown that they can discuss controversial or sensitive subjects calmly? Can you have intimate discussions with them? Karen says her father, an evangelical pastor, had a history of emotionally abusing her and her family of origin, so it wasn't a surprise that he reacted badly to news about Noah's gender identity. For twelve minutes, he berated her and her husband Kurt over the phone, so loudly that he could be heard from across the room: *It was as bad as we anticipated—or even worse.*

Jackie had a similar experience with a male relative who got loud and abusive as they discussed Rory, saying "terrible things"— and Jackie was the one expected to apologize for the sake of repairing the rift in her family of origin. That led to an "aha" moment: *This is always the way my family has done things, that someone acts abusive and the family tolerates the abuse, and they ask the abused to smooth it over and make peace.*

Even if there's no history of abusive language, ask, "Has my family shown they can handle talking about sensitive stuff?" Jake's family had no way to talk about their personal, relational lives. They expressed no interest in his romantic prospects, nor in any family member's relationships: *They just don't know how to talk about it. . . . We just don't have any established protocol in the family, so I think they don't know what to do.*

Evelyn's family had a history of avoiding difficult topics. Likewise, Leanne's family guideline was, "Let's not talk about it." The closest Leanne's mom came to acknowledging that her daughter is gay was to ask, "Are you okay?" when she learned that Leanne's partner's brother had AIDS. (She then asked, as follow-up, if Leanne's partner had AIDS.) In this first conversation with her mom about being gay, Leanne says, her mom still was elliptical: *She never says, "Are you a lesbian?," and I never said, "Yes, I'm a lesbian." She obviously understood that I was queer.* Leanne has impressed a new family guideline: "Let's talk," and she is explicitly out to her sister now, and they can talk frankly about her sister's gay son.

On the other hand, we see that Cole's parents, who asked him quietly and calmly if he was gay, accepted his denial (although they didn't believe it), and thought they were helping him treat depression when they sent him to a counselor. Ava says her parents respected the individual differences between their four daughters and supported them: *Mom and Dad taught us how to get along in society. Dad taught me how to work on my car. He taught one of my sisters how to work toward her theater interests. Both my parents really helped us develop our interests.* Kellie and Daniel, Jackie and Rory's dad, had been able to discuss, "What will we do if one of our kids is gay?" long before any kid came out. Their answer was "Love them."

Expressing Unconditional Love

Third, can your family express unconditional love? It's a stance that doesn't require intellectual understanding, just a commitment to the familial relationship. Ava's dad accepted her immediately when her mom could not: *He came over to me and hugged me and said, "I love you and I always will."* When Noah came out to her sister and asked, *Am I still your brother?* she replied, *Well yeah. You're just more you than you were before.* Her mom and dad were supportive from the first conversation, and Noah describes her mom as *over the top supportive. She is very effusive in her expressions of love for her children.* Cole's parents had a mindset of "You do you" even when Cole didn't. When Cole was talking with his dad after he came out, his dad told him, *"Well, we all knew that you were gay. We knew that you were giving it your last college try, trying to be straight for yourself or for us. But we knew you had to figure it out for yourself."*

Some family members who didn't understand their relative's declaration of a new identity brushed quickly past understanding to respond with love. Jackie regretted that her immediate response to Rory was to ask for clarification on bisexuality (*Can't you just date men, then?*). But she swiftly redirected when she realized that Rory worried that they were about to lose their entire family, including Jackie: *I immediately switched gears into, "I don't know how I'm going to figure all this out, but right now they need to know that I love them, and they're not losing me."*

Similarly, Daniel's first question to Kyra and Neve was, essentially, *What does this mean for my daughter Kyra?* but he ended that first conversation by expressing love and support. He and Kellie, having gathered Kellie's extended family in a big meeting, told the family that they didn't understand Kyra and Neve's situation, but they loved and supported them completely. Two of Rory's younger siblings told them, *I don't really know what I believe. I've been hearing things and it's not as clear as when we were growing up. I know I love you and I'll love you whatever you do.* Noah's paternal grandfather and Kyra's paternal grandmother fall into this category as well.

One of Kellie's "what ifs" concerns her deceased dad. He was, she and Kyra and Daniel agree, a larger-than-life character who set the tone in the extended family and was a source of unconditional love for all in the family. Kyra described how he protected her from bullying by her male cousins. Daniel described him as *a huge unifier of the family.* Kellie believes that if he were still alive, events would have unfolded differently: *He always ended up, as strong as he was, on loving people. My heart tells me that he would have said, "I worry about Kyra, I love Kyra, I love you all, everybody get over it."*

Evelyn feels that coming out revealed the conditional nature of her family of origin's love. She realized that her parents had always taken good care of them, providing all the material support they needed. But she had never felt unconditional love until she received it from her first girlfriend: *My mom was hard. She wasn't affectionate and my dad certainly wasn't. I just didn't understand why being loved was so bad.* Her parents' reaction to and rejection of her being gay made her understand that there were conditions on their love.

Get Protections in Place

Many of our friends, prior to and after coming out, distanced themselves from their families by living independently and insulating themselves with a nonfamily support system. Kyra and Neve waited to reveal Neve's gender identity until they got jobs and could move out of Kellie and Daniel's house. Rory moved out of their parents' house before they even began to consider that they were queer.

Ava speaks about the importance of asking yourself, "Who am I?" and coming to rely on yourself: *So a lot of my life was learning to rely on myself and knowing what I could do; and if I couldn't do it, learning how to do something different.*

Kyra and Neve put an emotional support system in place to keep Kyra's parents from having to fill that role: *We built our own circle of support so that if we lost our family support, we'd be safe. . . . I never thought my parents were going to be assholes, but I thought the extended family might be horrible to them. I thought that people might be horrible to my mom, and the further I could get away from them, the safer they'd be from their family.* Cole, too, built up his network of queer friends and used them as a sounding board before he came out. Jake found an institutional support system in the Gay Christian Network (now Q Christian Fellowship).

Where protections were not in place, our friends suffered. Evelyn was a teenager without resources to handle her parents' disappointment and anger. Many queer teens find themselves in Evelyn's situation, coming out while still a minor. Evelyn's family chose to receive her, belatedly and after a great deal of trauma to Evelyn, but other families of queer teens throw them out of their homes for good, making them vulnerable to exploitation. We are aware and so grateful that our friends who shared their stories for this book are still standing, as some of them endured harrowing rejections that could have led to devastating, even fatal, consequences.

Outcomes

It may seem harsh to point out the families that fell short by these measures, but I want to show the connection between a family's track record on those three factors and the probability of a decent response to coming out (that is, a response that does not diminish or impede the health and flourishing of the queer person at the center of the narrative, even if the response is short of affirming LGBTQ+ identity). The immediate families of origin of Cole, Noah, Rory, Kyra, and Ava each had a good track record on some combination of being open, talking calmly, and expressing unconditional love (with the exceptions of Ava's mom and Rory's dad). In the aftermath of coming out, those families, as reported by our friends, have intact and supportive relationships.

The immediate families of Jake, Evelyn, Marion, and Leanne had spotty track records in these three areas, as did the extended families of Noah, Rory, and Kyra, and we cannot describe those current relationships as supportive (with the exceptions of Leanne's sister and Marion's daughter).

This collection of stories doesn't present data to support this guess, but it makes me wonder: Is it only a revelation of queerness that would draw such negativity from some families? Or might there be any number of new self-understandings that would trigger hurtful reactions and lead to broken relationships in families that are already poorly equipped for difference, for change, for *the new world* Kurt's elderly dad recognized?

Challenge 4: Recalibrating Family Relationships

The last challenge our friends talked about was the aftermath of coming out. In their accounts, after a family member comes out and their family responds, both sides have decisions to make about whether to continue their relationship, and if so, on what terms? Everyone recalibrates their relationships: closer, more distant, new boundaries, new balance.

A Continuum between Two Poles

For our friends, it seems as if family members, by their responses, fell on a continuum between two poles: affirming and nonaffirming. In return, our friends responded by weighing an emphatic need to protect themselves—which they did with boundaries and buffers—against a deep desire for connection, sometimes emphasizing one more than the other.

The Affirming Pole

For our friends, family members closer to the affirming pole accept their queer family member, often want to learn more, and find ways to show their support. Kurt, Noah's dad, said of Noah, *I've got to trust that she knows herself better than anyone else. I think we're coming to learn that sexuality and gender are a lot more complicated than we've known.* Many other parents and siblings shared this view, whether or not they initially understood their family member's queer identity.

In addition, some made an effort to learn more about queer identity and issues. After reading several books on scripture and LGBTQ+ identity, Jackie, Rory's mom, concluded, *When I looked at the harm that is done, the pain that is endured, the unhealth in queer people's lives, all based on this one tiny thread of scripture, there's no way I could justify that.* Kurt keeps a list of books he can recommend to other conserving Christian parents whose kids come out. Kellie and Daniel have gone from being sympathetic to gay friends to being LGBTQ+ allies and activists, motivated by all that they've learned about trans identity and their love for Kyra and Neve.

Finally, affirming family members show their support not only through verbal acceptance but in other ways as well. Kurt, a biblical scholar, makes a point of coaching Noah with theological arguments for her to use in discussions with others. Kyra's paternal grandmother remade Neve's Christmas stocking, taking out the stitches of Neve's former name and re-embroidering "Neve." *I think that was the most powerful support in the beginning of our transition, from Grandma,* says Kyra. With relatives like this, our friends can emphasize connection over protection.

The Nonaffirming Pole

Nearer to the nonaffirming pole, our friends' family members expressed disbelief and hostility concerning their relatives' queer identities. Most of our friends responded, immediately or eventually, with hard boundaries, limiting access, and setting terms for future interactions. Karen cut off all contact with her dad after his twelve-minute tirade against Noah's identity over the phone, and she refused his later overtures. Noah and Rory continue to negotiate boundaries with their own and each other's extended families. Kellie was willing to decorate for a niece's wedding but refused to attend because Neve was not invited. You know it's a good boundary when you don't second-guess yourself or regret it; none of our friends did.

In a revealing response to such boundaries, two abusive and hostile family members, Noah's maternal grandfather and Rory's uncle, were surprised to find themselves cut off and demanded to be reinstated—as though they were entitled to these relationships entirely on their terms.

Our friends used a second strategy with family members toward the nonaffirming end: enlisting other family members as buffers. Cole described the benefits of buffers: *There was some turmoil when my cousins and my aunt didn't go to Christmas at my*

*grandma's a few years ago because I would be there with my spouse.
I didn't even know that at the time. What made me feel really great
about that is, I had so many people on my side that were fighting for
me. I love that I didn't even know that was going on.*

Jackie described the job as being the explainer, the educator,
with the extended family. She was frank about how hard it was:
*I had to keep Rory at the center, because ultimately it is their story,
it is their identity, and nothing I'm going through is as hard as what
they're going through. At the same time, it's kind of a helpless feeling, that I am paying an immense cost for something that I did not
choose.* The family members who served as buffers didn't talk about
how they coped with the task, so focused were our interviews on
the experiences of the queer persons at the narratives' centers; but
providing support for the buffers might be on the to-do list for any
queer ally or allied institution, like a church.

Between the Poles

Then there are the family members who fall between the affirming and nonaffirming poles. Jake's family as a whole occupies this
zone. He described a recent visit to his family as *the longest two
weeks.* He has come out to all his siblings; neither rejecting nor
accepting, they ignore his new identity: *I had to be this other person for them, this other version of Jake that they felt they've always
known. It was hard and exhausting, because I couldn't really be
me. It is so lonely, not having that family.* It's in this area also that
we find the family members who say they love you but can't remember your pronouns or your name or are uncomfortable with
your significant other.

What to do with this group? It's costly to walk away from a
shared history, from what Rory described as *memories of years of
kindness and generosity and family.* You also want to give people
a chance to move along the continuum, if you believe the tes-

timony of some of our friends who say that people can change. A mixture of love and hope keeps family members orbiting around each other, and our friends sought balance between protection and connection with this in-between group.

Boundaries help here, too. Noah, Jackie, and others draw lines around where and when they'll talk about, for instance, whether "gays" are going to hell and steadfastly refuse to indulge "But what's in their pants?"-type questions. They'll answer questions about general queer topics from someone they discern to be sincerely interested in learning but not otherwise.

Some of our friends also described their willingness to keep the (metaphorical) door open—that is, staying connected enough to some family members to allow for visits and discussion, while simultaneously and intentionally moving on with their own lives and support systems. Evelyn, for example, kept the door open and moved on at eighteen: *I just started doing my own thing and they had to accept it.* She made a life for herself separate from her family, working as a psych nurse, but did not cut her family out of her life. Intent on helping mentally distressed people and queer people, she said, *It's where I'm supposed to be. Everything I went through got me here.* In some sense her meaningful vocation has given meaning to the suffering she originally endured from her family of origin and has made it possible for her to find some measure of reconciliation with that same family.

Jake has a similar story: he maintains ties with his family but is enrolled in seminary with the goal of helping others who are struggling with the church's disapproval—a goal no one in his family of origin understands or supports—but Jake isn't waiting for that acceptance to live his life.

Marion, not out to most of her family, has found love and support in church and political activism. Describing a recent Pride event, she said, *All my communities collided. It was a beautiful swirl of color. This is how I feel now most of the time, that I have all the things that community is supposed to be.* Moving her chair from group to group, she thought, *As long as I stay here, as long as I stay physically in the places where I'm loved and accepted and I can just be, then I feel good.* The fullness of community makes possible her ongoing relationship with a family of origin that she hopes will never know who she really is.

(From material in my interviews that did not survive Katie's laser-focused editing, I know that it's at this point in their lives that some of our friends looked for queer-affirming churches. What they found when they went looking, and what churches could learn from their searching, could be a whole different project for us.)

There's a special category in this continuum from affirming to nonaffirming: the nonaffirming people you're stuck with because of your significant other. Evelyn spoke about how annoyed she gets at insensitive posts from her in-laws on social media, for example. She handles this with self-awareness, reminding herself of her ongoing fear that, after you peel the layers of family back, there's no unconditional love. In the case of newlyweds Noah and Rory, Rory's grandparents purposely misgender Noah. Rory is inclined to give them grace because of their shared history, but Noah lacks that history and thus is not inclined to let it go. Consequently, any interaction with that set of grandparents involves complicated negotiation of boundaries between the two of them.

Becoming an Ambassador, Pole to Pole

Inside and beyond the circle of one's family of origin are many people who fall somewhere along the continuum between affirming and nonaffirming. Some of our friends feel equipped and empowered to become ambassadors to them, traveling with confidence from their own absolutely affirming address to explain queerness to people who just don't get it . . . yet.

Many do it through their vocation, like Evelyn's work as a psych nurse who draws on her experiences to soothe distressed patients. Or Ava, a physical therapist, who made the decision to reply honestly to a patient about the wedding ring on her finger, telling the patient she'd recently married Leanne. Ava said, *They didn't know quite what to do with that, but they're still coming to see me, so I think we're okay.* Karen rejoices that her students know they can count on her: *They know they've got somebody who loves them for who they are, regardless of anything else. I feel that's important, to be there for that.*

Jake sees it as part of his mission to engage with people who ask questions in good faith. *I was able to cultivate enough respect in my friendships before I came out that people still extended that to me afterwards. They would be like, "But this is Jake, we know him." Even though I won't say it necessarily shifted people all the way over to affirming, they're not antigay anymore, which honestly I will take.*

Noah's dad Kurt continues to attend a conserving church on Sunday mornings where he regularly teaches an adult Bible study class and talks with the elders (congregational lay leaders) about LGBTQ+ inclusion. One elder, whose son came out, asked Kurt for reading resources and Kurt obliged. Later, the elder told him, *You really made a big difference for me. You were a life saver, and you opened up my mind to a different way of thinking.* Kurt notes that he's had conversations with other parents at that church whose kids have come out, acting as a sounding board and resource.

Jackie has conversations with a long-time friend, a non-affirming evangelical Christian: *I feel like there is hope that she will listen and reconsider. It feels like it's okay to let that go for now. She could change later.* Jackie also willingly answers questions about Rory's gender-queer identity from those she works with, if she thinks they are asking in good faith. Likewise, Kellie and Daniel have maintained solid friendships with conserving evangelical friends who love Kyra and Neve and ask about them. Kellie advises, *Be kind, because your heart may change over time.*

Finally, a Road Map for Everyone

Here's what we've learned in our careful listening. The work of all four challenges—accepting one's queer self, deciding to come out, coming out to one's family of origin, and recalibrating family relationships after coming out—can continue for years. And of course, coming out to one's family is one of many coming outs; queer folks have a lifetime of deciding whether to reveal their whole selves to their classmates, coworkers, clients, and church.

We know, too, that people change, requiring additional rounds of relational recalibration. People on the LGBTQ+ rainbow grow into their identities, sometimes with not-quite-there stops along the way, necessitating more vulnerability on their part (and offering more chances to family members to receive them with love). Members of the queer person's family of origin change, too, often moving over time to a more accepting position, requiring recalibration yet again.

This is why I'm drawn to the metaphor of a road map to describe this project: because all the stories from all our friends describe *movement*, and lots of it. What they needed most, and what they were able to create (sometimes with and sometimes against their families of origin), was a safe, generous landscape for all that movement. Their successful navigation of that landscape has worn paths that others can follow, and I've tried to capture the twists and turns they describe all along the way. I think their map matters, in more ways than I could have imagined before I heard their stories.

A Road Map That Matters

We began this project by promising to listen. We listened to what the coming-out experience was like for our queer friends and their family members, what helped them through it, and what shape their relationships settled into. We listened well enough to sketch a road map of their collective wisdom, marking what can happen along the way; what resources and strategies can be useful and where, as on any map, there be dragons. With map in hand, it's time for the "So what?" question: Who is this road map for? What difference could it make?

We hope these accounts make a difference for several groups of people we can imagine. For those just beginning this journey, whether a person discovering their own queerness or a family member of someone beginning to reveal their queerness, these accounts serve as a hope-filled guide to what's possible and why it's worth it, even if it's hard. The individuals and families we invited into this project were, as we've said, people who had on some level weathered the most difficult seasons of their respective journeys and had come to a place Katie calls "shalom"—not a romanticized or idealized version of a "happy" family but a settled place of relational equilibrium that our friends could peaceably inhabit. It's a destination that you can dare to hope for yourself, if you're new on this path.

For those who have already traveled this road with all its challenges and now ask themselves, "Could I have made this easier on myself?"—because that's a question we did get asked when we told people about this project—we hope these accounts provide reassurance. You're not especially bad at relationships and your family is (perhaps) not especially broken. It's a hard, messy, confusing experience for pretty much everybody, and there is no magic wand. It's quite likely that you did the best you could do, you made it through, and you're still standing—and that is worth celebrating.

For those who don't expect to ever face this experience, we hope these accounts spark empathy, and that empathy provokes support for LGBTQ+ dignity, rights, and inclusion. It's probably worth noting, however, that none of the families represented by our friends in this book expected the queerness that appeared in their lives. And the families whose relationships survived and deepened in the coming-out process were those who had a track record of openness to different experiences of being human. Perhaps by reading this you are preparing for the health and longevity of your most beloved relationships in a future you don't yet know.

The Truncated Road Map of "Queer Is Wrong"

We're also imagining another group that could benefit from these stories: all the people who pushed back on our friends and told them, "Queer is wrong." Such people are following a different road map than our friends. Theirs doesn't show everything they need to know; it doesn't show where the road is dangerously washed out or irreparably blocked, where the safe detours or the new highway can be found, or where the necessary rest stops are. Their map is truncated and thus mistaken, and it harms those who depend on it, even those who seem to benefit most from it.

First, it's mistaken. The "queer is wrong" map is used by those who subscribe to the cis-het patriarchy, believing or simply acting as if heterosexual, cisgender men are imbued with special qualities that grant them the right and power to determine how the rest of us should live. In this view, "real men" are at the top of the hierarchy and it's a cis-het-centric world. It's mistaken because the qualities that we value in human beings, the qualities that help us survive as a human family, are not tied to sexual orientation and gendered roles.

It's beyond the scope of this writing to take this belief apart piece by piece, but to those who say, "But the Bible says so," I'd refer you to an extensive body of work by biblical scholars, specialists in ancient languages, Christian theologians and ethicists, historians of our faith, queer theorists, and pastoral theologians who have done the painstaking and liberating work of dismantling outdated and incorrect "Christian" teachings that demand conformity to an ancient and cruel hierarchy that assigns and assumes the relative value of persons. Katie and I have been helped by the work of Matthew Vines, Colby Martin, William Stacy Johnson, and many others; we recommend a round of Google-sleuthing to find up-to-date resources for your own exploration.

Second, the truncated "queer is wrong" road map for navigating human formation according to strict categories and strata harms those who depend on it for their own status. A "real man," in the cis-het-centric worldview, is strong and successful, never admitting to pain or asking for help. But who is he when he gets sick, or loses his job, or loses his nerve? All human beings are vulnerable. When misfortune happens to him, a "real man" loses his identity and value. That map made it look like an easy path for those with high value in the cis-het patriarchy, but that path is actually quite difficult for them in ways we can measure. For quite some time now in the US, it's been the case that men die sooner, on average, than women. Current concern over "deaths of despair" highlights the increasing rates of death by suicide and accidental overdose for men who are unemployed and are suffering the pain of un-success—men who are, according to the map they inherited and carefully followed, *not* real men.

And of course, that "queer is wrong" road map limits the rights and opportunities of all kinds of people, not only queer people. Having black or brown skin, being a woman, inhabiting a disabled or differently abled body (and the list could go on)—"queer is wrong" diminishes many and thus harms many. In the final estimation, by limiting who counts and who contributes, it harms *all of us.* We live in a complex, uncertain world. We need creative solutions to big problems (climate change, income inequality, global pandemic, food supply chains, racism, species extinction, and so many more). We need everyone's contribution. We can't afford to discount anyone's experience or perspective.

The Beautiful Utility of a Flexible Map

Our friends, by sharing their stories, have sketched a road map that keeps them safe and connected and offers generous room for updating, by which I mean that the map can change when families change. And families do change—if we learned nothing more from listening to our friends, this would be insight enough. To wit:

Jackie at first resisted Rory's pushing her to an affirming stance. A friend at Galileo Church suggested Rory give their mom space and time, predicting she'd become one of Rory's strongest allies. The friend was right.

Kellie's elderly mom tries her best to get Neve's pronouns right, gets together regularly with Kyra and Neve, and supports invitations to family gatherings for both of them. Other members of Kellie's family reach out tentatively to Kyra and Neve as well.

After years of disapproval, Ava's mom apologized to her. What made a difference for her was being able to use her experience with Ava to help another family—made possible because Ava had not shut the door.

Between the time we conducted our interviews and the time we checked back with our friends to make sure they were okay with the way their stories would be told, a number of them said, "My family is further along now; we're in an even better place now than we were then."

The roads on this map we've made take various paths to a particular destination for each of our friends. Katie often talks to Galileo Church about what the world will look like when God gets everything God wants. These stories are not quite that, not quite the eschatological banquet of the prophets' imagining, but they hint at it.

Remember, I asked each interviewee at the beginning of our conversation to pick out a photograph of what their coming-out experience was like. I described those pictures to the reader as dark, messy, and confused. At the end of each interview, I again asked interviewees to choose a card that reflects their life now and their vision of their future. Everyone, *every single one*, picked out cards full of color, light, and movement. In their words, here's what that world is like.

Ava says she knows she's in a good place with her family: *We can be in the same room and laugh. I get to spend time with my nieces and nephews and their children. Leanne and I got married five weeks ago, and my nephew and his wife wanted their daughters to be at our wedding and so they came and they're just like, "Wow. It's such a big different world than we knew!"*

Jackie voiced how grateful she was for this reset to her life, which brought her and her kids to a better place. *Now my kids and their partners and I have family get-togethers, and we laugh, and we talk, and we enjoy each other. It really is like I thought my family was before, till it wasn't.*

Cole believes coming out made things better for him with his family: *All of a sudden, I was more honest with them and they saw into my heart.* He continued: *They were so excited for me. They could sense that I was in this new place in life; I was this new Cole that was really confident and unafraid.*

In our hearts, this is the world we want to live in, ourselves and our own families of origin. Our friends, in their vulnerability and courage, in their generous transparency, have given us a road map that everyone can use.

POSSIBILITY IS GOD'S PURVIEW

The Pastor's Conclusion

Katie Hays

Having known each other for a good long while, Susan and I know that one of the things we share in common is a tendency to wake in the night with worries. The monsters lurking under our beds spawned by this specific project have had to do with our right discernment of place and privilege. We worry back and forth over email (and over margaritas, IRL, when we can) about whether we are the right people for this work, whether it's appropriate for two cisgender, straight people to offer reflections about queer identity to the world.

As I said in my introduction, the act of testimony calls for a *listener*—someone to attend to the witness's account, to give ear to the story that unfolds as the witness strings together their lived moments into a sense-making, identity-forming narrative. But the act of faithful listening requires more than attention; what the brave witness finally requires is *belief*, an audience that not only hears but trusts the witness's experience as it is told to them.

Listening → Believing → Testimony

Remember the (male) apostles' disbelief when Mary Magdalene and the rest of the women gave their testimony to Jesus's resurrection: "Returning from the tomb, they told all this to the eleven and to all the rest. . . . But these words seemed to them an idle tale, and they did not believe them" (Luke 24:9, 11). There is always a risk associated with telling one's story; the subjectivity of testimony ("This is what *I* saw; this is what it felt like to *me*") leaves the witness extra-vulnerable, especially when narrating seasons of suffering. There is the vulnerability inherent in the event having happened, and the additional exposure of *saying* that it happened, right out loud to another subject (the listener) who may or may not find it credible.

And so Susan and I have positioned ourselves not only as listeners to our friends' testimony but as *believers*. They have told us what happened to them, what it felt like to live through, and how it feels now to remember it—and we have believed them. We could make a little diagram of the back-and-forth flow of trust between our friends and us, they in the first place trusting us with these deeply personal stories, and we in return trusting the stories they told us. That diagram would need to be laid over a prior picture of the Galileo Church community, where LGBTQ+ people and a whole bunch of other people exchange testimony and belief-ful listening all the time, so that Susan and I could borrow from the bank of trust that has built up over some years: "I trust you to hear and believe my story; you trust me to tell you the truth," back and forth, back and forth.

We hear from LGBTQ+ people that they have often not been believed, their experiences distrusted and discounted as if they were women on an Easter morning. Even as I write, the Texas legislature is stubbornly refusing to declare "conversion therapy" for LGBTQ+ persons illegal as a permissible form of mental health care, despite copious testimony of LGBTQ+ persons to the harm such quackery perpetrates on impressionable young humans. It seems to me that this kind of malpractice is but an extreme form of the more prevalent but subtler skepticism and denial queer people face from their families and churches—skepticism and denial that can easily become internalized, as many of our friends described taking a long time to come to terms with their own queer identity. Creating communities (families, churches) where LGBTQ+ persons' stories of self and identity will be believed is so much deeper than tolerance, acceptance, or even welcome. It is a practiced transaction of mutual trust, back and forth, back and forth, for as long as it takes to counteract all the condescension and distrust queer people have received from the rest of us for so long.

Now a funny thing has happened: because my coauthor and I have listened and believed, we have in turn become witnesses to our own experience of LGBTQ+ friends telling us about their families of origin. Their stories are now part of *our* story—not because we have lived their experiences but because our listening to their stories, with all our crying and commiserating and the real curiosity in Susan's gentle "Can you tell me more about that?," has *involved us* in their stories. We can testify now to what we have experienced by listening to them.

Because that's how it works: testimony is an invitation to the listener to know something she did not know before and to be changed by it. It may seem as if we invited our friends to do these interviews and tell their stories, but as soon as they started talking, they were inviting us to a new place of understanding. By believing their testimony, we said yes to their invitations, and we have been changed. We know things about how families of origin work that we didn't know before; we understand relationships strengthened or weakened by developmental difference in ways we could not have on our own.

What happens next is largely up to you, reader. Because Susan and I have become witnesses, and this book is our testimony, and you are our listener. The question for you is, do you believe what we've told you? And if you do, what might it mean for you?

Testimony as Evangelism

We've been careful, Susan and I, to avoid the white-lady-of-a-certain-age trap of telling anybody/everybody what they *should* do—though Susan's analysis highlights some of the times when our LGBTQ+ friends dispensed wisdom won by hard experience. We've tried to keep our commitment to being *descriptive*, in other words, rather than *prescriptive*. But I'd be lying if I said I hadn't thought at all about what this book of testimony could mean for our readers.

The whole set of stories reads, to me, as *evangelism*. It's both *good* and *news*, which are the necessary ingredients of evangelism. And the best evangelism is the breathless, excited reporting of something that has happened to you, something that has changed everything for the better, something you think might be good for other people, too. It's testimony, in other words, offered in trust, in the hope of being heard and believed.

Our friends' testimonies are brimming with good news of at least two strains that I can see: first, wherever you are, you are not alone; and second, wherever you are, you won't be there forever.

Wherever You Are, You Are Not Alone

Coming out is such a useful expression for the queer person who decides to externalize and articulate their sexual orientation or gender identity, because the term forever recalls the experience of "being in"—that is, the extreme isolation of knowing you're the only person in the whole, wide world who knows who you really are; and of being misunderstood, misgendered, misrepresented, everywhere except in your own mind. So many of our friends described years of existential isolation. Some of them, decades.

And when a person starts coming out to their family of origin, that isolation sometimes extends to the family members who know the queer person's queerness as a closely kept secret that fragments families along an invisible border between those who know and those who don't. It's lonely, even when a few people are together in that loneliness.

Over some time, the queer person and their family-of-origin settle into a new normal, keeping an internal ledger of who knows and who doesn't, who approves and who doesn't, who's safe and who's not, learning to respect each other's tolerance levels for compromise, and figuring out the steps to a complicated choreography for holidays and birthdays and weddings and funerals, all the occasions that call families of origin into proximity of each other, even when distance is the preferred method of ensuring safety for the LGBTQ+ beloved. *Every family's combination of these details is different*, just as the shape of every family's good-enough shalom is different.

Despite those differences, the good news here is that whatever arrangement you and your family of origin are settling into, you are not alone. Within just our tiny sample, we've heard stories of families who have arrived at destinations all over Susan's roadmap, from lovely scenes of widespread familial harmony around the full inclusion of LGBTQ+ relatives, to queer individuals with only one or two allies among their blood kin, and every configuration in between. We are hopeful that everyone can find some kinship (pun intended!) between their family and the ones whose stories are included here. The details may differ, but the destination will feel . . . familiar (pun intended?).

That's good news, true evangelism, because solidarity is a good gift. It is how God's own Self expressed God's love for us—by becoming like us, in Jesus, God's own "Me, too!" to the whole human family. If any of the stories presented herein gave rise to a "Me, too!" from you, we would count it as an evangelistic win.

Not that we count wins in evangelism. But you know what I mean.

Wherever You Are, You Won't Be There Forever

Susan mentioned this in her concluding essay, but it bears repeating: when we sent the edited narratives to our friends for their approval, some of them as much as two years after they talked to Susan, many of them wrote back to say, "Sure, but so much has changed since then! Shouldn't we update?" Indeed, at least one of our friends was convinced we had fictionalized their story by rewriting it in someone else's voice. It sounded more tentative, less resolute than they remembered ever feeling, so far were those experiences from their current state of mind. When I insisted that every sentence was taken directly from an exact transcript of their interview, they searched their memory and agreed by email: *The events are true but it almost feels like it happened to someone else. Maybe that's why it feels so surreal—I read some parts of it and it is so different from who I am now. It's hard to recognize that person as myself.*

Another interviewee emailed to say that they noticed, *after reading the story, that things have somewhat changed for the better. Some things remain the same. But it is absolutely the truth, and is a fair description of exactly what happened. It's the truth, or it was, and I'm not ashamed of telling the truth.*

Another friend offered a truly lovely reflection they wrote recently, after attending a wedding where many members of their family of origin were present, including lots who are nonaffirming and have even been blatantly cruel to the queer relative. There was a time when our friend couldn't imagine that their attendance at such an event would be possible, but it proved to be an opportunity for a kind of experiential reconciliation, where no one names the conflict or its resolution, but everyone understands that healing is happening. Or, if not healing, at least a cessation of wounding. Our friend wrote, after having a delightful time that night: *The standard we demand of family members in order to share a meal with them and enjoy their company is not as unattainable as*

I once thought, I'm learning. Family doesn't mean anything goes, but it means some grace. . . . My family has a wide welcome, actually. Wider than I once thought. I'm grateful.

It's such a Christian idea, that our identities and relationships are not set in stone. We are intended to grow and change. We are intended to recognize and enjoy growth and change in ourselves and in others. "Sanctification," the church has called it: *And all of us,* the apostle said, *with unveiled faces, seeing the glory of the Lord as though reflected in a mirror, are being transformed into the same image from one degree of glory to another; for this comes from the Lord, the Spirit* (2 Cor. 3:18).

Susan says our friends have drawn for us a "flexible roadmap," one that changes as families themselves change. This might be the best news of all, the most welcome evangelism: our friends' testimony that the only constant in their relationships with their families of origin is change. "From one degree of glory to another" might be a little flowery, but the changes they describe have been almost all for the better.

This is the best news because the possibility of change opens (or reopens) our capacity for hope, particularly the hope that the isolation induced by queer identity formation (for some) and queer identity articulation (for some) is not the end of the story. Relationship is possible. Better relationship is possible. Being heard and believed is possible. Being loved for the person you are, and the person you are becoming, by the people who knew you first and imagine that they know you best, even if they don't know you at all right now, is possible.

And possibility is God's purview. This is the good news; this is our testimony. And now it's yours if you want it.